wildly
sophisticated

wildly
sophisticated

A Bold New Attitude for Career Success *

Nicole Williams

A Perigee Book

A Perigee Book

Published by The Berkley Publishing Group

A division of Penguin Group (USA) Inc.

375 Hudson Street

New York, New York 10014

Copyright © 2004 by Nicole Williams

Text design by Tiffany Estreicher

Cover design by Ben Gibson

Cover photo © by Getty Images/DTF Productions

Perigee trade-paperback edition: February 2004

ISBN: 0-399-52947-0

Visit our website at www.penguin.com

Library of Congress Cataloging-in-Publication Data

Williams, Nicole, 1970–

   Wildly sophisticated : a bold new attitude for career success / Nicole Williams.—1st ed.

     p. cm.

   ISBN 0-399-52947-0

   1. Women—Employment—Psychological aspects. 2. Achievement motivation in women. 3. Attitude (Psychology) 4. Self-actualization (Psychology) 5. Success—Psychological aspects. 6. Vocational guidance for women. I. Title: Attitude for career success. II. Title.

   HD6053.W49 2004

   650.1'802—dc22

2003063255

Printed in the United States of America

10   9   8   7   6   5   4   3   2   1

For Isabella

Table of Contents

Acknowledgments

This book simply wouldn't have been possible without the support, direction, and commitment of the following: my in-house editor and writer Cheri Hanson, for her extraordinary talent for bringing stories to life on the page, her ability to call "bullshit," and for her willingness to take the leap with me each and every day. My agent, Kim Goldstein, for her tenacity and her commitment to make my unthinkable, thinkable. For the team at Penguin, Perigee: My editor, Michelle Howry, who fought for this book and provided extraordinary feedback, guidance, and support. John Duff, for his enthusiasm for the project and his ability to see and share in the "Big Picture." Liz Perl, Craig Burke, and Rebecca Crowley for their commitment to spread the word. Con Buckley, for being such a sage, dedicated, and loyal adviser. Paul Jarvis, for bringing our visions to life through his designs. Sandra Parker, for her wisdom and for showing me how to walk the path of truth. Praveen Varshney and Paul Grehan for investing not only in my dream, but in me. Doreen MacKenzie Sanders, for reminding me "nothing comes from nothing."

I'm especially thankful to all my family and friends for their love and support. To my grandparents, Doris and Ernest Smith, for their unconditional belief in me. My mom, Linda Williams, who inspires me with her integrity. My late grandfather, Donald Williams, for sharing his legacy in writing, and my nana, Eileen Williams. To Shane Williams, for being my brother and sharing my life.

To my dad, Bernie Williams, for constantly challenging me. To my parents-in-law, Leo and Jeanne Comesotti, for being ready with a bottle of champagne and for continually supporting our lives. My friend and "muse" Jennifer Wolfe Hannay for her loyalty and creative vision—this wouldn't have been possible without her. My heartfelt thanks to my best friend, Jennifer Little, for sharing her light, and "Mom Little" for always being on my side.

Both this project and I have been surrounded by an amazing group of Wildly Sophisticated women who have inspired much of the material in this book. First and foremost, thanks to all the women who offered their confessions, shared their stories, and joined us for Drinks After Work. Lisa Johnson, my business partner, friend, and missing link. "Roxy Roller" Zurbuchan for being the glue that keeps us all together. Kirsten Tisdale, my beloved friend and mentor. Heather MacKenzie, a constant source of strength and inspiration. Kelly Alison, for always sharing what's "right." Lisa Butler, for seeing our friendship through thick and thin. Michelle Herbert, for being the sister I always dreamed of and for sharing Julianne and Matthew. Denise Rossetto, who I don't get to see often enough, but who I love knowing is out there in the world.

Last, but never, ever least, to my wonderful husband, Roy Comesotti, for showing me what commitment, loyalty, trust, and love really mean. I bask in your magnificence and I am so grateful for your presence in my life.

1

Are You Wildly Sophisticated?

Am I a Wildly Sophisticated Woman?
The Power of Attitude

On the last day of high school, one of the most feared and respected teachers circled the classroom choosing adjectives to describe each of his students. Considerate with some, tactless with others, he reached my desk and hesitated.

I froze caught somewhere between fear and anticipation. A lifetime passed before he finally said, "Nicole, while this seems a contradiction in terms, you are what I would describe as wildly sophisticated. There are no better words to describe your combination of passion and refinement, energy and contemplation."

I didn't hear the adjectives he selected for the rest of the class. I was too absorbed in the phrase—Wildly Sophisticated. Never had I heard those words used together before, and never would I let them go. If there's such a thing as a defining moment in a person's life, this was mine. For reasons I still don't understand, those words ignited a potential I didn't know I had—and clarified a vision of something and someone I wanted to become.

Just as those two words changed my life the minute they left my teacher's lips, your life shifted when you picked this book up off the shelf. If you already have a sense of what Wildly Sophisticated means, if you somehow know that Wildly Sophisticated is intended for you, I promise you this—it is.

Wildly Sophisticated is not only an expression to describe what you already are, it actually gives you a framework to bring your abilities, your dreams, and your passions to life.

Individually, the word "wildly" suggests risk, energy, boldness, vivacity, self-promotion, and fearlessness, while "sophisticated" incorporates refinement, simplicity, commitment, elegance, and respect.

Put together, "wildly" and "sophisticated" become a way of being—an attitude with which to take on the world.

As you build and manage your career, know this: There is no single formula for success. There simply is no definitive path. Instead, it is your attitude—your willingness to learn, to experience, to enjoy the process—that ultimately leads to achievement.

The Attitude Advantage

Why is your attitude so important?

I've met young women fresh out of the most prestigious schools in the country who just can't seem to get a break. And then I'll meet others who, without finishing their degrees, have taken their career by the horns and have risen to the highest executive ranks. More than talent, more than skill, more than IQ, more than experience, your attitude is what gives you the edge.

If there's one thing I've come to learn as a career manager it's this: Your attitude is the single most important, most significant contributor to your career success.

With today's world of work in a constant state of flux—job descriptions, opportunities, and expectations changing in the blink of an eye—attitude has become *the* critical foundation for creating career success. In a dynamic and challenging job market, you need to be enterprising and creative in order to reach your potential.

And this is the crucial point—you have tremendous potential. Your potential lies in your attitude, and that attitude has a name: It's called Wildly Sophisticated.

The Quest for Success

The rules of work have changed forever, and they will continue to evolve. In the face of such constant change, the questions become infinitely more important than the answers. These are the nine questions you'll need to build the career of your dreams, and Wildly Sophisticated is the attitude you'll need to answer them.

Are You Wildly Sophisticated?

Who Do You Think You Are?

What Are You Revealing?

Are You Up for a Challenge?

Are You Prepared?

Are You Willing to Accept Help?

Are You Ready to Give This Everything You've Got?

Do You Have to Choose?

What Are You Waiting For?

> Within the word "question" is a beautiful word—quest.
> —Elie Wiesel

While I can't answer these questions for you, I can help you create your own solutions. And more than just questions, you will also find strategies, tips, ideas, and inspirational confessions to move you into action. Start with the questions, apply your Wildly Sophisticated attitude to find the answers, and as you do, you are living your very own Quest for Success.

Career development is a Quest—an adventurous expedition. While you can plan, you can't predict. While you can try with all your might, you can't control. While you can dream, you can't experience without action. What you *can* do is choose, and the most important choice you have to make is your attitude.

Your attitude is your compass on the Quest—your guide. You will experience so many unexpected detours, challenges, and triumphs, and more than anything, your perspective will influence your experience of success. Your answer to the question, "Am I a Wildly Sophisticated Woman?" is the foundation you will need to answer the other eight succeess-building questions in this book.

These are the questions I've asked (and still am asking) to build my career—and my life. The thing is, it's the process, not the results, that holds the key to learning. You succeed. You fail. You fall down, you get back up, you keep asking the questions, and you keep searching for the answers—on your own terms. This is how you create success beyond your wildest dreams.

This book is about you—your attitude and your choices. What do you want to bring to this process, and what do you want to get out of it?

Use your Wildly Sophisticated attitude to answer the questions that follow in this book and the result? You will be unstoppable.

Making It Real

Okay, so you're thinking, "no shit." Attitude is everything. I'm not telling you something you haven't heard before. But here's the difference: I won't leave you hanging. I'm actually going to define what this attitude is. You will see, feel, and understand how the words Wildly Sophisticated can build extraordinary success.

Don't get me wrong. The word "attitude" is tough to explain. I built an entire business around the Wildly Sophisiticated attitude, but until recently even

> I wouldn't dream of working on something that didn't make my gut rumble and my heart want to explode.
> —Kate Winslet

I hadn't truly defined it—not for lack of trying. I could feel what Wildly Sophisticated was, I knew it when I saw it, but I had yet to really describe it. For months, my business partners and I would sit around asking, "OK, so what makes Reese Witherspoon Wildly Sophisticated and Pamela

Anderson not so much?" But then a TV production executive asked me, almost as an afterthought, "So what exactly is Wildly Sophisticated?"

The moment had arrived. Time to finally nail it down.

THE WILDLY SOPHISTICATED COMMANDMENTS

Start Personal to Be Professional

I've heard the "need to separate your personal and professional life" debate more times than I care to count, and I don't buy it.

We spend up to 70 percent of our waking life at work. If that isn't inspiration enough to think seriously about getting into the game, consider what work gives back to you. Work provides an extraordinary opportunity to realize your potential and fulfill your dreams. Work is a means by which you can challenge yourself, express who you are, push your limits and boundaries, discover yourself, and test your values and integrity. Work offers you the opportunity to make a contribution, to put your stamp on the world through your best efforts.

"Achievement doesn't come from what we do, but from who we are. Our career is an extension of our personalities."

This quote from Marianne Williamson is brilliant. Career development is all about you. To create success, you start with yourself—your unique set of talents, skills, and abilities—and essentially bring the best of you to your work. Now, this is the important part: Work doesn't define you; you define work. It is not a luxury or a privilege to find joy, passion, and fulfillment through work—it's a choice. It's a commitment you make to yourself.

Not personal?! That is my work, my sweat, and my time away from my kids!! If that is not personal, I don't know what is!!
—Erin Brockovich

Career success starts and ends with you. As a Wildly Sophisticated woman, you are committed to bringing the best of yourself to your work. You are continually striving to understand yourself better—your strengths, weaknesses, passions, values, goals, fears (yes, Wildly Sophisticated women have fears)—and you can apply this knowledge to enhance your professional performance. You use your career to both explore and express yourself.

Learn, Learn, and Then Learn Some More

I've been watching an interesting phenomenon for a long time now, and it highlights why learning is such an important part of the Wildly Sophisticated attitude. I call it the "got it all together" disease. It looks something like this:

> *Three women are having drinks after work. Two are meeting for the first time.*
>
> *"What do you do Theresa?"*
>
> *"Oh, I graduated with honors in law from Harvard, finished a summer semester abroad in London, and now I'm with Fisher, Brackman and Price. I have the most amazing and supportive co-workers, and I just adore my boss. I love my work."*
>
> *"How about you Patricia?"*
>
> *"Well, I just graduated with a masters in economics from Oxford and came back to New York to work for the United Nations. I'm so excited and stimulated by my work. I can't imagine doing anything I love more."*

I'm the third woman in the crowd—and I know the truth. To start, Theresa didn't quite graduate with honors, in fact, she passed by the skin of her teeth. And the supportive co-workers she's described are three men who have essentially relegated her to the filing room. Patricia, on the other hand, had one of the loneliest experiences at Oxford. She often questioned what she was doing there, and now, with a full-fledged "career" in one hand and massive student debt in the other, she's wondering if she shouldn't have become a doctor.

One of the first things I noticed when I launched a career management business is that many of my friends—the same friends who, months earlier, convinced me they didn't have a career struggle in the world—would suddenly open up and chat intimately about their professional challenges. Sure, we're happy to spill everything about our failing fitness regimen, the fight we had with our boyfriend, even the most private details of our sex lives. But shift over to careers, and hell, we've got it all together. We love what we do, and it's all working beautifully. Every single one of us awakes refreshed, ready to tackle another day of fun, fulfilling work. Sound familiar?

> **I believe that everything happens for a reason, but I think it's important to seek out that reason—that's how we learn.**
> —Drew Barrymore

Here's the deal. Not knowing, uncertainty, admitting you don't have it all together—that feels risky. As young women, we're in the midst of a high learning curve. Somewhere along the way, we've all learned to equate our careers with our self-worth. If our work isn't everything we want it to be, what does that say about us? Admitting there are struggles can make us feel vulnerable and inadequate. But we don't have it all together (at least not all the time), and pretending that you do is not going to help you, it's going to hurt you—and all the other young women around you. Pretending that you know it all is immensely dangerous, because it stifles the flow of learning.

The first step is admitting that you don't have it all together all the time and that you actually have something to learn. The second step requires a level of willingness to take action. Sometimes, when we are setting out on our Quest, we feel unstable and we'd rather focus on what we *do* know than on what we don't. Exposing the gaps in our knowledge can make us feel vulnerable. But whether it's through mentorship, our own mistakes, or through a friend's objective perspective, it's our willingness to learn that makes us Wildly Sophisticated.

As a Wildly Sophisticated woman, you are

> **Learning is not attained by chance; it must be sought for with ardor and attended to with diligence.**
> —Abigail Adams

always looking for opportunities to stretch, push your limits, and expand your mind. You're not afraid to admit you don't know, and you actually revel in your "unknowing" as a critical source of learning. The Wildly Sophisticated woman understands that knowledge and growth are critical to creating career success, and regardless of the outcome, you will walk away with lessons learned.

Embrace Your Excellence

Right from the start, we need to agree that excellence is not the same as perfection. I watch a lot of us get caught up in this trap. On one hand we are ready to get out there and make our mark on the world. On the other, we want to have it all down pat. We want to expose our perfect selves to the world, highly coiffed and qualified, not the still-floundering, not-quite-ready, slightly shaky, sometimes-scared selves we really are. Many of us are waiting to feel perfectly prepared, perfectly skilled, perfectly ready—and this drive for perfection actually limits our ability and our willingness to get out there and start living the Quest.

I have some very important news for you: The best of what you've got and who you are at this very moment is enough. Waiting to feel perfect is a losing battle. One of the best ways to beat the perfectionist trap is to think about it this way: Perfection is externally defined, while excellence is internally defined. You know when you have tried your hardest—no one else can judge your best efforts. On some days, excellence means getting your ass off the couch; on others, it means working into the night to put the finishing touches on your proposal. The thing with excellence is that you can't trick yourself, and doing any less than your best actually erodes your sense of confidence and your ability to succeed.

> **Perfectionism is the voice of the oppressor.**
> —Anne Lamott

Being Wildly Sophisticated is not about conforming to someone else's standards. It's about putting forward the best of what and who you are.

Nothing Comes from Nothing

It's a standing date. Every three months, my friend Maria and I get together for dinner. The conversation, dynamic on every other level, always comes back to the same thing—she wants to build a business of her own. Now, I love Maria, and I believe she can do anything. The problem? She's doing nothing. It's a hard juxtaposition. I'm in the business of helping young women, so friends regularly confide in me about their career distress. Although they're looking for an embrace, what they clearly need is a kick in the ass.

The time had come. With love and support in my heart, I prepared to punt Maria out of stagnation. The heart-to-heart I had to have with Maria is not a lot different than the one you will have with yourself numerous times on your Quest. There is a time to talk, and there is a time for action. In my experience, we're motivated by a combination of hope or fear. And although hope is often where our Quest begins, fear is often what compels us to actually get moving. One of the most effective ways you can inspire action is to ask yourself, "What will my life look like if I don't try?"

The great news is that there's a point where not acting on your dream starts to drive you crazy—usually long after you start driving your friends and family up the wall. There will be many times along your Quest when you are on the threshold of bringing your dream to life. You have a vision, however blurry, of your potential. This vision is like a leaky faucet driving you to distraction, and finally you can't ignore it anymore. Once you fully recognize and acknowledge your dream, you have no choice but to act.

The Quest for Success requires action, which can be especially challenging when it's

> My dad always used to tell me that if they challenge you to an after-school fight, tell them you won't wait—you can kick their ass right now.
>
> —Cameron Diaz

attached to a personally meaningful goal. Being Wildly Sophisticated starts with an attitude, but this attitude only gains true power through meaningful action.

The choices are yours to make. If you don't like your current job, change it. If you know you are destined for more, go after it. Wildly Sophisticated women don't wait for opportunities to come to them. They take initiative and create opportunities for themselves. The Wildly Sophisticated woman knows that to obtain career success, she is ultimately responsible for going out and getting it. She understands that action builds confidence, that confidence builds momentum, and momentum builds success. Get moving.

Stand Out from the Crowd

Afraid of insulting me, my boss tentatively asked if I would consider meeting an image consultant. Rather than being humiliated, I was elated. Let's put it this way: It only takes one case of mistaken identity—when a man of comparable age and status confuses you with the secretary and asks for his coffee to be delivered with cream *and* sugar—to fully embrace the idea of an image overhaul. As a twenty-eight-year-old executive, I was coming to understand the importance of professional image, and I was all about improving mine.

With visions of makeup counters and shopping sprees and the conviction to retract all those nasty thoughts about my boss's frugality (she must have *really* thought I needed this), I prepared to meet my Transformer. After waiting ten minutes in the lobby, I was greeted by a creature I believed to be a woman. Standing over 6 feet tall, she towered over my 5'2¾" frame. And with mitts to rival Michael Jordan's, she quickly engulfed my hand to assess the firmness of my shake.

> **Normal is not something to aspire to; it's something to get away from.**
> —Jodie Foster

The "date" started at a local restaurant. Have you ever dined with someone whose sole purpose is to assess your eating habits and dining etiquette? It's more than a little disconcerting. The Transformer, clearly sizing me up with a tangible sense of resentment and indifference, constantly asked questions just as I was about to start chewing. When our lunch was finally over, I was still hungry and had an important question of my own: "Where are we going shopping?"

No such luck. We headed back to her office. The Transformer pulled out what I'm sure is the same color chart my mom and her girlfriends used back in the 1980s. Holding the wheel to my face, she scrutinized me closely before deciding I was a "winter." As such, I should integrate more fuchsia and perhaps turquoise into my wardrobe. Bad news. Everything I own is black, gray, beige, or white. My idea of playing with color is a red handbag and matching shoes. Before I could protest, she asked me to stand.

The deadly serious makeover charade played on. The Transformer sighed as she offered a final assessment.

"Now Nicole, as a young woman, you have a lot working against you. People will, quite rightly, think of you as inexperienced. If you want to stand out from the crowd and command respect, you will need to do a couple things. My first suggestion is that you wear heels—high heels. As you have seen in working with me today, height equals influence. My other suggestion? You need to cut your college hair. Long hair on a woman conveys sex, and if you want to be taken seriously, you need to look serious. Short hair is serious."

Speaking of serious, I started to wonder if she was seriously crazy.

In the end, my Transformer was seriously disappointing. She didn't turn me into a more glamorous, commanding version of myself. I didn't get any great clothes or awe-inspiring makeup advice. Bottom line? I wasn't at all transformed. But I did learn an important—and Wildly Sophisticated—lesson.

Without question, as a young woman you want to stand out from the crowd—but you need to stand out on your own terms and in your own unique way. I've come to disagree with the Transformer on a few levels: I still have my college hair, and I don't think you need to deny your youth to make an impact. The very fact that you are a young, vivacious, and industrious woman is where your

> The way I feel about music is that there is no right and wrong. Only true and false.
> —Fiona Apple

differentiation begins. As a young woman, your fresh perspective is one of your fundamental advantages. Don't underestimate your ability to innovate and to generate unique approaches to countless challenges and opportunities.

So what does a Wildly Sophisticated woman look like? I bet you can identify her when she walks into a room—and it's not about fashion *per se*. She radiates an energy and confidence that is at once elusive and undeniably present. As a Wildly Sophisticated woman, you have a personal style that is distinctly yours and yours alone. You express your style through everything from the words you use to the clothes you wear. In the highly competitive world of work, you know how to stand out from the crowd, and you understand that you are your own best asset, quirks and all. You make the room, your working environment, your networks, and your career your own. You are willing to be different in order to follow your heart, and outside of the crowd becomes a place you're comfortable going.

Expect Nothing but the Very Best

Slinging boxes onto skids in the back of a paint factory is not my idea of a good time, but it was the reality of my life during the summer months of my university years. I would amuse myself by reading something, anything, in the newspaper on my designated fifteen-minute break and spend the next two hours escaping boredom by debating the issue.

One afternoon, my mental debate-fest was interrupted by a shifty kind of guy asking if I would like to be cooled off. I looked up to see his hands filled with two cups brimming with cold water. While in the context of a backyard BBQ I might have said yes, his beady little eyes were telling me no. As he launched the water directly onto the front of my white T-shirt, I couldn't help but notice that while I was cooling off, he was heating up.

I'd like to tell you I walked off the job that moment (although I should have, I didn't). Instead, I went home that evening feeling a bit sad but mostly ashamed of myself for not standing up to the mistreatment.

One of the most important things I learned that fateful day—and, quite frankly, keep on learning throughout my Quest—is that you don't need professional status or power to have standards for yourself and others; you need personal strength. As a Wildly Sophisticated woman, you begin to understand that wanting and expecting the very best is directly tied to what you actually receive.

Integrate what you believe in every single area of your life. Take your heart to work and ask the most and best of everybody else, too.

—Meryl Streep

If there is one message you can adopt on your Quest, it's this: Expect nothing but the very best—both from yourself and from others. I meet a lot of young women who work in shitty jobs with abusive bosses and who somehow believe they're lucky to have the work. And I meet even more young women who don't realize that taking extra time to proofread a memo isn't about a misspelled word, but about the pride you take in your work. The most challenging part of this Wildly Sophisticated fundamental is that it's cyclical—to create standards for yourself you have to believe you're valuable, and to feel valuable, you have to have standards.

Not having personal standards might feel easy. It means you don't have to stand up for yourself and others, it means you don't have to fight for more, and it means you don't have to define your worth. In fact, lowering your personal standards is the most devastating thing you can do to yourself, and it will impede your Quest for Success more than anything or anybody else.

Get Over Yourself

My niece, Renée, greets me at the door wearing pink tights and a matching pink tutu. Before I can even give her a hug, she ushers me into the living room, where the entire family is seated. "Watch my tape!" she cries, as her mom presses PLAY on the VCR. Renée's first ballet recital. As the music starts, we see fifteen three-year-olds shuffle onto the stage. Some dance with their brows furrowed in concentration, while others stop and wave to their parents in the audience. One girl starts to cry and runs off stage. Another sticks her finger firmly up her nose.

As we watch her taped debut, Renée begins skipping and leaping along to the routine right there in the living room. I look over at her and smile. She doesn't care what we think of her dancing—she's just having fun. She loves to dance (and she definitely loves her pink tutu), but most of all, she wants us to share her excitement. No fear. No self-consciousness. No pretensions.

I left our personal recital with a firm belief that that little Wildly Sophisticated Renée had the secret to success we all need to remember Get over yourself. True success requires a sense of adventure, and it means you can't take yourself too seriously. You are going to make mistakes. You are going to embarrass yourself. You are going to fail. Who cares? Most everything is eventually forgiven and *forgotten*. Remember this, too, in the face of success: You might be all the rage one week and a distant memory the next. Think Shannon Doherty and get over yourself.

> I take my career seriously, but I don't take myself seriously.
>
> —Kate Hudson

Career development is a lifelong Quest, and it is infinitely more fun when you step out of yourself to help others and gain some perspective. As a Wildly Sophisticated woman, you need to be able to laugh at yourself and the sometimes precarious positions you will get yourself into. To appreciate the adventure and excitement that makes career development worthwhile, you need to remember one essential thing: Get over yourself.

❄   ❄   ❄

Wildly Sophisticated is an attitude to guide you through triumph and failure, encouraging you to welcome the questions and giving you a foundation to create your own solutions.

Wildly Sophisticated was a gift. My teacher gave me a new way to describe an attitude and a way of moving through the world. It doesn't matter who or where you are—Wildly Sophisticated is the attitude that somehow makes you want more from your life, and more importantly more from yourself. When my teacher called me Wildly Sophisticated, he opened the door to my future.

My goal is to open that door for you.

2

Who Do You Think You Are?

Defining Yourself

For more than two years, I had been dreaming of a company that would revolutionize the words "career development." Imagine a Martha-style overhaul of the working world. Think glamour, commitment, and confidence. Turn 180 degrees away from punching a time clock and instead, use your career to help build a rich, fulfilling life. Filled with vision and excitement, but scared of losing my place on the corporate ladder, I kept my day job and toiled at my project in the wee hours of the night.

Finally feeling bold, I shared my secret dream with a colleague. She suggested her father, a prominent and respected businessman, might be able to help. I sent off the business plan and anxiously awaited his feedback.

A few nights later, I spotted my colleague's father at a charity event and approached him excitedly. He warned me that his comments were critical. In my head, I understand that criticism is a part of the process, but my heart was screaming, "Run, run away." He opened by saying, "So you want to build a business?"

"Absolutely," I nodded and took a large sip of my gin martini.

"Your plan is interesting, but I have to ask you this . . . Why you? There have been lots of people, older and more experienced than you, who have failed. Who do you think you are?"

Recovering quickly for the sake of appearances, I downed the rest of my martini, smiled graciously, and said, "Great question." Excusing myself to the ladies' room, I approached the mirror, hoping for a glimpse of the woman who was determined to make this project succeed. Too wrapped up in all my covert excitement and drive to bring this project to life, I had forgotten to ask myself the most important question of all—who do I think I am?

Who Do You Think You Are? It seems like such a simple question. It's almost something we take for granted (living with ourselves and all), something we don't consciously think about until we're asked. When faced with the question, I experienced a mixture of feelings ranging from defensiveness to absolute fear.

When I got home the night of the charity event, I crawled into bed and lay there considering my options. I could hole up and cry through the next day— my first and most natural inclination. Or I could use this question as a catalyst, a means by which to move forward. As truly frightened as I was, I knew I had not answered the question, and until I did, I would not be successful.

Who Do You Think You Are? is the critical starting point. If you are not living the life you desire today, this is the root of your problem. The great thing about career development is that it's all about you. The not-so-great thing about career development is that . . . it's all about you. Success depends on your ability to answer to the question Who Do I Think I Am?

> I don't like it when people sugarcoat things for me. I'm the best judge of my own work.
> —Reese Witherspoon

How can you expect to create a career reflective of your passion, values, and talents if you don't know what those are?

Understanding the concept that career development starts and ends with you is fundamental for creating success. Others may influence, others may inspire, and others may guide you part of the way, but ultimately, the only person who can determine whether you can do something is you. There have been times when someone thought I did a great job at something, but in the back of my mind I thought, *If they only knew what I could actually do.* There were also times when I gave a project everything I had to offer, only to be told that everything must change. The reality is, deep down you are the only person who knows if your Quest—your efforts, your career, your life—is truly reflective of who you think you are.

In many ways, exploring the question Who Do You Think You Are? is both an investment and a risk. Many of the young women I challenge to answer this question hesitantly ask, "What if I discover I'm on the wrong track, or finally face my dreams and have to admit I'm destined for more?" I don't know that I can imagine anything worse than lying on my deathbed, after working the majority of my waking life, only to discover my career in no way, shape, or form reflects who I think I am. How about you?

There are three critical things to remember as you read this chapter:

- **You define success.** You are going to be infinitely more successful if your career reflects you—your talents, passion, and dreams. If you want to be more successful, on your own terms, learn more about yourself and take the time to figure out what success actually means to you.

- **You are dynamic.** Who Do You Think You Are? is a question you will have to come back to many times throughout your career. Your vision and understanding of yourself today will change as you grow and evolve—and so should your career. Career development, just like personal development, is a lifelong process and commitment.

- **You are worth it.** This is your investment to make. Career development is challenging work—don't kid yourself into thinking you will coast into the career of your dreams. Be willing to invest the time and effort to understand yourself better.

This chapter focuses on helping you explore and answer the question, Who Do You Think You Are? This knowledge will support you in living a life and creating a career that reflects your desires, talents, and values. Once you figure out how you want to define yourself, all your other career decisions can be made to further this vision of you and of your success.

GET HONEST WITH YOURSELF

We face so many different—and often conflicting—messages about who we are and especially who we *should* be. Magazines, parents, co-workers, partners—everyone has his or her own vision for our lives. This chapter focuses on helping *you* evaluate and answer Who Do You Think You Are? for *yourself*. Starting with an honest admission of the confession you've been afraid to reveal, you'll explore your passions, talents, and core values. You'll think about who you admire and define what work really means to you.

> Harboring dark secrets. Lying. Pretending. Trying to be someone you're not. All these things are weights that prevent you from reaching your greatest potential. In order to fly, you have to get the weight, the garbage off of your wings.
> —Oprah Winfrey

Before you can even begin to answer the question Who Do You Think You Are? you need to commit to be honest with yourself. You're scared you will never figure out what you actually want to do with your life. You know you have the potential to try harder, but you can't seem to push yourself to the next level. You're frustrated thinking the process is taking too long. Every Monday morning you wake up with dread in your heart at the prospect of facing another week at work. Answering the question Who Do You Think You Are? requires you to examine your life with honesty and without judgment. Make a pact with yourself to be as honest as possible—even if you don't like or are afraid of what you might discover.

At this stage, I don't care if you're ready to tell the world about your secret fears and mistakes, but I will tell you this: When you don't trust that your truth is enough and start to exaggerate your accomplishments, deny your truth, or lie about reality to *others*, you lose track of *yourself*—the very essence of what you need to create career success. Start exactly where you are and commit to telling the truth. It's the foundation you need to answer this and every other question in this book.

Confession Time

Think Natalie Portman–like combination of beauty and brains. Think top of her competitive MBA class. Think promoted to VP within "Big Five" consulting firms before age thirty-five. Think marathon runner, skier, and excels-at-everything athlete. Think DKNY suit with matching Prada handbag and shoes. Think mentor!

Kirsten is one of those women who has everything—and I mean *everything*—going for her. She commands respect and admiration from everyone she works with. She is infinitely more sophisticated than wild and was ordained with the stature, luck, and power that put her in the ranks of Gwyneth Paltrow.

On one fateful afternoon, Kirsten and I met at a board of trade meeting. On our walk back to our respective office buildings we decided to grab coffee. Sitting at a small table, we talked about one of her current projects. I could sense something was a little different. Kirsten's usually confident demeanor seemed slightly worn.

"Nic," she asked, "do you ever get scared?" Before I could respond, she continued. "Sometimes when I'm about to start working on a new project," she said, "I can't help but wonder, is this where I get found out?"

There it was—Kirsten's Career Confession.

We all have them. Our confessions are those nagging secret fears that live deep within us and have the potential to keep us from our dreams. Once revealed,

strategy*

Write your own Career Confession. If you don't know where to start, think about these questions: Where are you? What are you afraid of? What is holding you back? Do you have a secret concern, hope, or fear that needs to be acknowledged?

Remember: Career Confessions require a safe space. Whether you write your confession in a secret journal or share your confession with a trusted friend, make sure your confession is held in a place where you can tell the truth about yourself.

If you enjoy this process, you might want to write a weekly or monthly Career Confession. The process allows you to honestly reflect on and keep track of your fears, secrets, and uncertainties, all of which will be an important part of your Quest for Success.

these personal truths free us to face up to and deal with our reality. Confessions are a way of acknowledging and working through the journey—the challenges with the successes. Every one of us, independent of how successful we are, has confessions. They are what make our lives interesting, dynamic, and exciting.

Even Kirsten, who appeared to have it all together, admitted she felt afraid. In a way, her confession relieved me, not because I wanted her to feel scared, but because confessions have this funny way of making us think "I feel that way, too." Kirsten seemed peaceful after she finished speaking—as if her confession alleviated the burden of her secret. She didn't reveal her feelings for my benefit; she did it for herself.

That's the thing—confessions are about you and for you. I don't care if you write them, speak them, or draw them. Just make sure you articulate the truth—the root of what's making you feel frozen, what's making you afraid, or simply what's separating your real life from your dreams. However you choose to do it, confessions provide another opportunity to learn about Who You Think You Are, to see where you want to go, and to explore fears that might be holding you back.

I've heard the Career Confessions of young women from around the country. They're sometimes startling, sometimes sad, sometimes proud—but always honest. I've included Career Confessions in this book because they show you that although your Quest is uniquely your own, we all share common fears, obstacles, and moments of bliss along the way. If you're feeling stuck, I can guarantee about a million other young women feel they are in the same boat. Relax and give yourself a break. Take comfort in knowing that everyone struggles, and, with time and effort, we all find our own answers.

Impostor Syndrome

Kirsten wasn't the first person I ever heard talk about feeling like an impostor, and she definitely wasn't the last. Of all the little secrets we have lurking in the closet, this is one I hear time and time again. Regardless of profession, age, or success level, women everywhere suffer from a perplexing phenomenon—the Impostor Syndrome. It's the sense that you've somehow tricked people into believing you are more than what you feel yourself to be. Sound familiar? Take heart.

If, at the heart of Who You Think You Are, is a desire to push your limits, learn, explore, and try things that scare you, the Impostor Syndrome isn't likely to ever vanish completely. Feeling like you are bluffing is *not* the same as lying, especially when you have the desire and ability to work your way through to a solution. As Kirsten reminded me a few weeks ago, "You build a sense of confidence that you're going to figure it

> Sometimes I don't feel like the person I'm supposed to be. I don't feel like I deserve any of this.
> —Mena Suvari

> I think self-awareness is probably the most important thing toward being a champion.
>
> —Billy Jean King

out. That's what it's all about. At the beginning of your career, you feel like you're bluffing, and that's disconcerting. You feel like you're not being truthful, but in fact, you are."

That said, if you agree to spearhead a new client account in Spanish and the only words you know are *por favor* and *gracias*, you've moved beyond the syndrome and you have truly become an impostor.

PINPOINT YOUR PASSION

It's the most exciting process to witness. A young workshop participant will be lamenting how she can't find her passion, when she is asked, "What topic of conversation do you absolutely have to participate in?" Suddenly, she's got ten, fifteen, twenty answers. Her face lights up, and she lists off ideas faster than she can speak. Inevitably, her brow soon furrows. She stops. "But this is just about conversation. I need to find my P-A-S-S-I-O-N."

Career Confession

WHAT? WHERE? HOW?

I'm driven, I'm motivated, and I'm ready to go. I can accomplish anything—anything! There's just one problem. I don't have a clue what I want that "anything" to be. I have nightmares that I'm an Olympic sprinter before a race, but when the gun fires, my feet get stuck in the starting blocks.

Heather, student

People talk about Passion with a capital P. They say the word with reverence, like you need to hold a séance or consult a Ouija board to conjure it up from the Great Beyond. From books to magazine articles to reality TV, finding our passion has become our new religion. It's a solemn, serious mission we accept with the gravity of a search for the Holy Grail. But once people start answering simple, basic questions about their lives and loves, I can't tell you how often they finally unearth the root of their passions.

> **Passion is not an event, but an energy; and it's an energy that exists in all of us, all the time. The question is not whether we have it, but whether we access it and how we channel it.**
>
> —Derrick Bell, *Ethical Ambition: Living a Life of Meaning and Worth*

And here's the most important thing to remember (this is crucial!): *Passion* is not a synonym for *magic*. When you tap into your passions, you're not going to feel the world slide into slow motion, see fireworks explode in your head, or

strategy*

PASSION QUESTIONS

If you are having trouble identifying your passions, here are a few questions to ask yourself:

- What am I good at? (If you're not sure what you are good at, ask yourself what you enjoy. Most often we enjoy what we excel at.)
- What gives me energy?
- What do I have strong feelings or opinions about?
- What am I known for? What do I do better than anyone else in my circle of friends or family?
- What am I talking about or doing when others observe me "come to life"?

✳ **One-on-One**

What Works for You?

I feel like shit before I have a shower. My energy drops like a lead balloon around 3 P.M. I have the propensity to argue with anyone who reminds me of my dad. If I get too hungry, I alternatively snap like a dragon or burst into tears. Too much information for you, but these little tidbits are what make my life work.

One of the most important things you can ask and learn about yourself is, *What Works for Me?* You have different ebbs and flows of energy during the course of the day. You have habits, things about your daily life that make you feel alternately comforted, energized, inspired, and deflated. There are certain kinds of people you are going to have a distinct response toward. These are the kinds of things you need to know about who you are. Based on what you learn, create some structure in your career around what you know works for you.

---

hear Pavarotti singing the soundtrack to your life. Passions are everywhere; they are the topics you debate with your friends, the films that tell stories you cherish, the way you feel when you take care of your four-year-old niece. Passions are big, small, dramatic, and subtle. They're everywhere you are.

If you're feeling desperate and near certain that you are the only one without a passion, I want you to think about a great first date. The options are endless (really, they are). You've finally decided to commit to dinner. The food, the conversation, the connection—all fantastic. What do you do now? Do you call him forty-nine times in the next twenty-four hours? Do you create a wedding scrapbook and choose names for your unborn children? Do you push him for a commitment and insist he answer your question—Are you the one? Only if you want to ensure there will never, ever be a second date. Apply this same logic to your search for passion. Play the field, put in the time, and enjoy the process—

but don't flounder around in desperation. Allow your passions to emerge naturally. Passion, just like love, isn't something you can force.

TALLY YOUR TALENTS

I just got off the phone with a young woman who has a phenomenal talent—Julia is a natural photographer. She's in the midst of a career transition and has been "indulging" herself by taking photos. It's something Julia's always loved, and it comes exceptionally easy to her. Word is spreading about Julia's evocative portraits and her great eye for composition. People are asking for her services. They want to "book" her weeks before a family event. Most importantly—they want to pay her!

When Julia asked for my opinion, I suggested that her next step was looking pretty clear. Here was a viable business literally knocking on the door and asking to come in. I knew she also had the business sense and the market position to really make this fly. But Julia was skeptical:

"Nic, photography is just my hobby. I can't make a career out of this—*it's too easy!*"

For me, Julia's story illustrates the principal difference between your talents and your skills. Sure, Julia knew the difference between ISO 100 and 400 and the ins and outs of shutter speed. But those are skills she learned—skills any one of us can learn. Her real talent is looking through a camera lens and pressing the shutter at exactly the right moment. Skills are learned, but talents are natural. In fact, your talents often feel so natural that you might not even realize they are talents. They simply feel like an extension of you.

Although the list of talents in the Talent Inventory strategy is certainly not exhaustive, it will help identify the areas—in your everyday

Most people die with their music still locked up inside them.

—Benjamin Disraeli

strategy*

Using this list for ideas, create an inventory of your talents.

Organizing	Inventing
Motivating	Teaching
Managing	Strategizing
Leading	Negotiating
Counseling	Investigating
Building	Clarifying
Designing	Investing
Performing/entertaining	Telling stories
Communicating	Planning
Analyzing	Making decisions
Synthesizing	Entrepreneurial

■ For each talent you select, describe a situation in which you utilized this talent to its fullest. Use as much detail as possible. How did it feel to explore and use your talent?

■ In relation to each talent, ask yourself if your current job allows you to fully experience and realize your talent.

■ If you are not utilizing your talents in your current workplace, are there ways in which you can begin to integrate your talents into your work?

life—where you naturally excel. You can learn a lot about who you think you are by pinpointing your natural talents and abilities.

Find Out What They Need?

Rob Sullivan, author of *Getting Your Foot in the Door When You Don't Have a Leg to Stand On,* suggests this strategy for discovering and identifying where your talents lie. Simply ask yourself the following question:

When people come to me for help or advice, what, specifically do they need?

Rob also suggests that as part of your self-assessment, you should ask people who know you well what they see as your strengths, talents, and abilities. Sounds a little awkward, doesn't it? Nothing like cozying up to your closest friends and family members with a conversation starter like "So tell me . . . what exactly do you like about me?"

But Rob's definitely onto something here. Those who we hang with or are related to often see things in us that we simply don't identify in ourselves. Ask people who will take your request for feedback seriously, and who make you feel comfortable with the discussion. Above all, avoid the natural temptation to dismiss their answers out of disbelief or even modesty. If your talent was really nothing special, your friends or family wouldn't have identified it in the first place.

WHAT DO YOU VALUE?

It seems everyone has been shown a list of values and has been asked to tick off or rate their "Top Ten." You know the drill—loyalty, family, success, wealth—and the list goes on. But the identification and expression of your values doesn't come from a list of words. I've known more than a few people who proclaim to anyone who'll listen how much they value honesty only to turn around and

strategy*

Sit or lie back, close your eyes, and remember a time in your life when you felt joyful, exhilarated, and happy. Think about the situation in as much detail as possible. Where are you? Who are you with? What are you doing? How are you feeling? Open your eyes and write down all the things that came to mind. Whether it was playing with your sister, laughing, winning an award, or being promoted, write down the details without overanalyzing. Once you are finished, take a look at what you have written. By recalling a time of true happiness, your key values are exposed.

List all the values you can come up with from that experience. The following list might help get you going. Once you have your list, read it over and think about how you can more thoroughly integrate these values into your everyday experience. More than anything, our lived experiences feed our values. If you value generosity, for example, sign up to be a Big Sister.

What works equally well is to go through the same exercise but start with a memory attached to a time in your life when you were sad, lonely, or distressed.

Acceptance	Pleasure
Humility	Excitement
Ambition	Family
Responsibility	Honor
Sense of belonging	Independence
Success	Generosity
Wealth	Power
Wisdom	Discipline
Honesty	Pleasure
Privacy	Friendship
Peace	

construct a lie of mammoth proportions! Your values live in your experiences, in your actions, and in the way you treat yourself and others.

> The ultimate measure of a man is not where he stands in moments of comfort and convenience, but where he stands at times of challenge and controversy.
>
> —Martin Luther King Jr.

More than a mental laundry list, your values are something you live. One of the most critical misunderstandings I've seen with clients is that they confuse their values with opinions or ideas about how they should live their life. This is really important, because your values—your real, true, lived values—are a direct link to your behavior. If you're not being honest with yourself, the values you think you have, your actions, and ultimately your goals will be way out of whack. If, for example, you think you value financial responsibility but you don't have a budget, spend beyond your means, and are afraid to request that long-overdue raise, don't kid yourself—and don't be surprised next time you hit the ATM and you find you're out of cash.

Discovering and defining your values is an essential component in figuring out Who You Think You Are and will help you evaluate opportunities and make both personal and professional choices. For this strategy, you'll need to find some quiet time in which you can concentrate on yourself without distraction.

WHO DO YOU ADMIRE?

Who's kidding who? Exploring who we think we are is challenging work. All that self-reflection and navel gazing can be exhausting. Sometimes it helps to leave the mirror and look at the people around us. Think about the people you admire—friends, celebrities, or pretty much anyone you find intriguing. What makes each person interesting? How are they unique? Your answers say a lot about who you are and who you want to be. And you thought this was a break from the internal exploration!

Inspiration

I'll never forget my first conscious brush with inspiration. Some friends and I were waiting to see Sarah McLachlan at a local club. When the lights dimmed and the curtain raised, there, in the middle of the open stage, stood a young woman with her acoustic guitar—the opening act. Her first tentative strums

strategy*

FINDING INSPIRATION

■ **Who are your Great Ones?** These are the icons (living and dead) high on your mental pedestal—from Oprah to Gandhi to Ella Fitzgerald. From the very beginning of my "working" life, I have always had two photographs on my desk, one of Maya Angelou and the other of Toni Morrison. In both pictures, Maya and Toni have their hands raised in passion and their faces are lit up with delight. I have kept these pictures with me throughout my career to inspire and remind me what great work is meant to look and feel like. Think about how you can bring the inspiration of your Great Ones to your everyday life.

■ **Who are your Everydays?** Your mom? A caring friend? A teacher? It could even be the man running your local newsstand who inspires you with his amazing work ethic and good humor.

Once you've identified your Everyday, tell her all about it! Write her a quick (or not so quick) note of thanks. Let her know specifically how she has influenced your life. Your words of appreciation will inspire your inspirer to inspire—if that makes any sense!

■ **Who are your Believers?** These are the people who have always said, "Yes, you can!" They support your dreams and were met with an initially shaky voice, but as the music emerged from her, the sound became increasingly strong and powerful. I sat back in awe—this young woman, obviously in one of her first performances, was emerging to greatness. I was at once humbled and inspired.

Actively seeking inspiration is an empowering way to envision and realize your potential. Surrounding yourself with great people and circumstances will consistently fuel your desire to excel. Inspiration not only allows you to draw upon the success of others, but it's an amazing way to explore and discover Who

encourage you to pursue excellence. My business simply would not be if it wasn't for a group of seven women who believed I could do it. Your Believers are not a collection of fair-weather friends who are only willing to support you through the good times—these are the people who, through thick and thin, rally behind you, willing to carry you to the finish line when your legs are too tired to walk one step farther. Share your dreams and passions with a hand-selected group of people who believe in you and are willing to support you over the long haul.

■ **What are the most inspiring moments you've experienced in your life?** These are the moments when the world stands still. They leave you breathless, bring you to tears, and raise the little hairs on the back of your neck. In one of those blissful moments of absolute joy, I felt compelled to write a note of thanks to the universe. "Thank you, thank you, and thank you, again. This is the most amazing, challenging, glorious, joyful, creative, exciting process I've ever lived." Okay, a little over the top, but I swear I had been having such a bitch of a time that I really needed to savor the moment! It's not that I couldn't conjure up the image in my mind without the note, but there is something about seizing the moment and actually capturing it. Whether it's a snapshot of a spectacular sunset, a note, or a conscious mental photo, find ways to capture and keep your inspirational moments in a safe place you can call on again and again.

You Think You Are. Have you given much thought to what and who inspires you? As with all aspects of being Wildly Sophisticated, your answer will be highly personal. You might find inspiration in nature, in supporting another young woman debut her work, in reading a great book, or in conversations with your best friend.

Birds of a Feather

You've seen the picture—the one with Chelsea Clinton nestled between Gwyneth Paltrow and Donatella Versace. Somehow this simple photo made us all think a little differently about Chelsea. Although I don't know much about the former first daughter, I would not include her among the fashion elite and then . . . this picture. What was she doing with Gwyneth and Donatella? Better yet, what were they doing with her? Regardless of their relationship, their association prompted people to think of Chelsea in a new, more fashionable light.

strategy*

R-E-S-P-E-C-T

- Make a list of five people you admire and respect.
- Reflect on each of these people and describe the characteristics, attributes, and abilities you most admire about them.
- Examine the essence of the words you have chosen to describe each person. In most cases, we choose characteristics, attributes, and abilities that are more about us than they are about the person we are describing. What we admire in others is often what most resonates within ourselves.

This photograph is a powerful reminder of the birds of a feather phenomenon. The people we associate with influence the way people perceive us. Choose to associate with people who reflect who and what you are.

WHAT DOES WORK MEAN TO YOU?

Is this a trick question? A paycheck, of course. For many of us, money and security are the bottom-line necessities, and that's okay. Unless you were born into

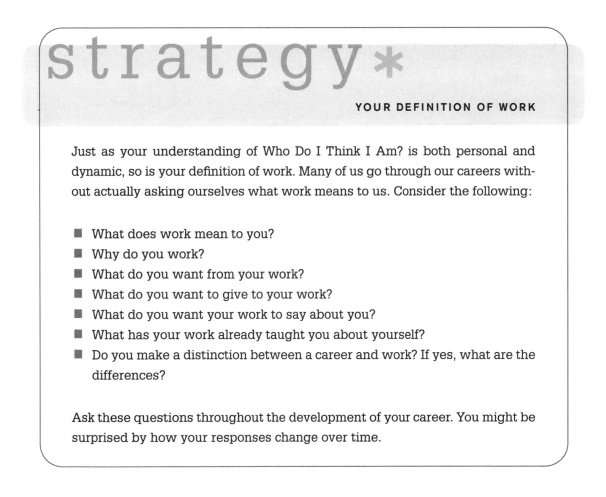

strategy*

YOUR DEFINITION OF WORK

Just as your understanding of Who Do I Think I Am? is both personal and dynamic, so is your definition of work. Many of us go through our careers without actually asking ourselves what work means to us. Consider the following:

- What does work mean to you?
- Why do you work?
- What do you want from your work?
- What do you want to give to your work?
- What do you want your work to say about you?
- What has your work already taught you about yourself?
- Do you make a distinction between a career and work? If yes, what are the differences?

Ask these questions throughout the development of your career. You might be surprised by how your responses change over time.

riches (and sometimes even if you were), work isn't optional—all the more reason to make it something you love, something that fires you up and makes you eager to face the day. The interesting thing is that so many of us don't think past what we're going to do and where we're going to do it. If you really want to build a satisfying career, you need to dig a little deeper. The strategy on page 33 will help you explore your ideas about work—what it means, what it can do for you, and what you can give to your working life.

REINVENT YOURSELF

Nicole's New Year's Resolutions

2002	2003	2004
Lose five pounds	Lose five pounds	Lose five pounds
Get toned arms	Get toned arms	Get toned arms
Save money	Save money	Save money
Cut out the caffeine	Reduce the caffeine	Buy shares in Starbucks

If your fear of exploring yourself resides in the fact that you're afraid you won't like what you learn, I have the greatest news: You can change. There is no shame in not being where you want to be on your Quest for Success. You might have found through this chapter that there are things about yourself and your career that you want to change and reinvent. From the superficial (a real haircut, professional-looking shoes) to the soul-searching (explore my passion, work to my potential), we all have things we'd like to upgrade. True reinvention requires a number of things—many of which I will discuss throughout this book—but the most important

> A career is a portfolio of projects that teach you new skills, gain you new expertise, develop new capabilites, grow your colleague set, and constantly reinvent you as a brand.
>
> —Tom Peters, business leader and author

is a vision, a vision of Who You Think You Are and who you want to become. This mental image isn't just a destination. It's also a reflection of where you are now. You already have the foundation. Your vision will give you the clarity to move forward.

I think I've probably reinvented myself three or four times now, if that's what one calls it.
—Sarah Brightman

Write Your Own Script

I have a bright, airy home on the island of Capri and a loft in Manhattan. My six-year-old daughter is playing at the foot of my walnut desk. Friends and family gather for animated dinners around the large, circular kitchen table. I'm peaceful but invigorated, committed but in control.

This is my life, all right—ten years from now.

How do I know? Several years ago, I spent a listless afternoon reading through my old college-and-beyond journals. While I had to dig through all the melodrama (talk about a great way to get over yourself . . .), I slowly began to see that ten years ago, I had unconsciously planned the life I was living right there and then. The fuzzy vision I had pieced together in those journals had actually become the template for my life. My salary, my responsibilities— even my marriage—had all been laid out in those pages. I started to think about where I would be in another decade. I decided to write the script that would lead me forward; only this time, I would approach it consciously.

I know, I know. *I've heard this before,* you're thinking. Maybe you're yawning or rummaging through the fridge for a snack. This is touchy-feely stuff. But I promise you won't have to play "inspirational" music laced with seagull cries or pull out a cloth-bound journal decorated with rosebuds. Please—please, give this strategy a try. This self-conscious, entertaining little exercise will change your life.

strategy*

What is your vision of Who You Want to Become? Write a letter to yourself today as the person you are aspiring to be. Describe your life. Where do you live? Describe your home. How do you spend your days? Describe the important relationships in your life. Be as explicit as possible. Make it tangible. You're more likely to create success if you have a truthful, authentic, and dynamic vision of who you are and who you want to become.

The thing is, as you start writing about your collection of Versace couture gowns and the private jet you're chartering to Ibiza, something very interesting starts to happen. All those fantasy scenarios start revealing the truth. You want an island retreat? You want to run your own company? Clearly, you're looking for some peace and a sense of control. As long as you're being honest with yourself, the vision you paint for the future is actually a true portrait of who and what you are right now. And if you're afraid to really think about the future, afraid that you'll be disappointed by the ultimate reality you find ten years down the road, forget about it. I promise, if you set a course for yourself grounded in the truth of who you think you are, there will be *nothing* disappointing about your future.

❅   ❅   ❅

It wasn't long ago that I ran into my friend's father—the businessman who asked "Why you?" that fateful and faith-testing night. There was a part of me that so badly wanted to brag about my business, my book deal, and my thriving career. It took everything in me not to taunt him with "I told you so." But the reality was, in facing him again I was humbled. I knew I had nothing more to do than thank him for asking the question that changed my life. I realized that when it comes down to it, the only person you need to be accountable to is you.

You know who you are. That's all you'll ever need.

3

What Are You Revealing?

Expressing Yourself

MEETING AGENDA—Monday, May 12, 1996

1. Board of Directors meeting
2. United Way fund-raising campaign
3. Expense budgets
4. Dress code

I still get embarrassed when I think about it. I'm in the first year of my "career," feeling powerfully professional. I skim over the weekly meeting agenda and stop dead in my tracks—*Dress code*. The rising flush on my face, sickness in my stomach, and a quick glance down at my miniskirt was all I needed to confirm this little item for discussion was meant especially for me.

It's a solid eight years later, and regardless of the fact that I actually help women create their professional image for a living, I can still see the agenda in my mind's eye and remember that unique moment of discomfort. You know the feeling. It's a nagging sense that something's not right—you're uncomfortable in your own skin.

Self-expression is all about authenticity. It's one thing to understand who you think you are. It's another thing entirely to express that knowledge through your clothes, through the way you communicate, and through your decisions and your choices. Understanding requires thought. Expression demands action.

Like it or not, people are constantly assessing you. It's happening at work, on the bus, and while you order your lunch. But wait, this is a good thing. Why? Because you're in control. You can choose to reveal and express anything you want about yourself. You're energetic, creative, and articulate. Don't you want the world to see that, too? Self-expression—through language, clothes, communication—is your opportunity to flaunt the very best of what and who you are.

My miniskirt felt uncomfortable because it put my thighs center stage, instead of my brains and my professional competence. We've all been there. Something you wore or said or didn't say just felt "wrong," and that sense of discomfort can slowly eat away at your confidence. It's distracting. It takes away from your focus, and from all the incredible skills, ideas, and energy you bring to your life and your work.

> I've always wanted to be a spy, and frankly I'm a little surprised that British Intelligence has never approached me.
> —Elizabeth Hurley

Still think it's too much trouble? *Good God,* you're thinking. *I'm lucky to get out the door in clean clothes that match, and now you want me to reconstruct my entire professional image?* But here's the best part: Authentic self-expression is actually *freeing.* When the way you write and dress and the choices you make flow naturally from Who You Think You Are, it gives you a sense of power and confidence. And you know as well as I do that there's nothing better than someone who oozes confidence. It's sexy, it's appealing, and it's definitely Wildly Sophisticated. Confident self-expression frees you to tackle the stuff that matters. Really, who wants to spend half the day tugging on a too-tight skirt or worrying that you told your boss a dirty joke? You've got better things to do.

This chapter builds on your understanding of Who You Think You Are.

We'll explore what makes you distinct and discuss how you can express that individuality in your working life. From your unique personal history to your clothes and the values and boundaries you uphold, your career offers an incredible opportunity to express yourself with flair and confidence.

PART ONE
DEFINE WHAT MAKES YOU DISTINCT

Pink. Christianne Amanapour. Queen Noor. Sarah Jessica Parker. J. K. Rowling. Venus Williams. Alanis Morissette. You need only hear their names to conjure up adjectives to describe these high-profile women. From Gwen Stefani's killer abs to Jodie Foster's demand for privacy and her understated style, these women have all created a level of distinctiveness based on Who They Think They Are. Everything from their personal style to the unique way they express their talents, these women have created a distinct image that we all identify as unique to them.

Creating and expressing individuality is critical for building success—and not just for big-name stars in the entertainment industry. You can captivate your own workplace, industry, and career with an image that is both powerful and unique to you. From your Signature Story to your professional image, you have the opportunity to create a level of distinctiveness that reflects Who You Think You Are.

Step Up And Step Out

You don't need to be a seasoned professional to get out there and shine. You are young, vivacious, energetic, and full of new ideas—think key differentiators! Bring this expression of Who You Think You Are to the table. Don't

strategy*

Unlike Jennifer Lopez, most of us do not have the luxury of a team of people to help create our personal brand. We have to create our own unique style.

Being distinctive in your career is essential. Consider this: When you are one of fifty applicants for a job or one of thousands auditioning for the perfect part, how will you stand out from the crowd? What makes you memorable, irresistible—distinct?

- Take some time to review your list of talents, the feedback you received from your friends and family, what you know about yourself based upon who you attract, and your values (essentially, everything from Chapter Two).
- Choose five to ten attributes, talents, characteristics, and values that most resonate with you. What feels most like you?
- Think about how you can package these attributes, talents, characteristics, and values in a way that is unique to you. Your "package" is like your signature. It's the image people immediately visualize when they hear your name.
- Need some ideas? Although only you can create your distinct "package," look around you. There are sure to be some people in your life who have a unique image they are recognized for.

wait a moment longer to develop a unique niche and voice within your career and your industry. As a young woman, you already have innovative ideas and fresh perspectives. Never underestimate what you have to contribute right now.

Here are a few ways to increase your profile:

Speak Up

Contribute to conferences or panel discussions. If your palms are already getting sweaty, practice public speaking by giving a toast at your best friend's wedding or join a speaking club such as Toast Masters International. Still too daunting? Challenge yourself to say something—anything—at your next staff meeting.

Do It Differently

Whenever possible, take a new, creative approach that capitalizes on your talents and your innovative perspective. Everyone else hands in dull, bullet-point reports? Make yours a slick, well-laid-out document complete with charts and quotes. You don't have to go crazy. Just look for opportunities to express yourself and do the unexpected.

Write It Down

Draft an opinion piece for your local newspaper or write an article for your industry trade journal. If this is too daunting, start by suggesting a story for the company newsletter, or better yet—write it yourself.

Show Up

Conferences, trade fairs, presentations, and workshops—go to where the movers and shakers do their thing, and learn from the best. You never know what you're going to learn or who you'll meet, so just show up. Take a deep breath and introduce yourself. Simply and authentically compliment your role models and pass on your business card.

Join In

Sit on a board or join a group in your field. You'll make amazing connections and get great leadership experience. Becoming active in an organization requires time, but the payoffs are huge.

> People laughed at the way I dressed, but that was the secret of my success: I didn't look like anyone.
>
> —Coco Chanel

Skills like fund-raising, event planning, public speaking, and financial management have the potential to turn volunteer experience into paid work. Seek out the groups that provide the best fit with your professional and educational goals.

One last note: As you step into the spotlight, understand that there are nervous, jealous critics waiting in the wings.

A new promotion still hot in my hand, a competitive colleague decided to invite herself into my office. She sat in the chair across from my desk, looked me straight in the eye, and said, "I'm sick of you being the ray of sunshine around here." It was one of my first lessons in the price of success.

If there's one thing I can promise you, it's that as you start to shine there will be people who will perceive your achievement and distinctiveness as threatening. Armed with their own potent fear, they'll try to pull you into their professional neuroses. Don't play their game. If you are working from your own dreams, desires, and standards, you have nothing to fear—and you definitely have nothing to apologize for. As an ambitious, Wildly Sophisticated woman, you will be the ray of sunshine—don't let anyone rain on your parade.

Tell Me About Yourself

We've all faced this question—and we've all blown it. Does this sound familiar? Someone says, "Tell me a little about yourself . . ."

Your response:

"Well, um, I just finished my education degree, and I'm, well, in truth, I'm working at the Y because I can't get into an elementary school. I kind of like kids, actually, I guess I like them a lot. I did a whole degree in education, didn't I? Anyway, yeah, I'm sort of a teacher."

Nervous laughter.

It's not so much that we screw this up, but we miss a great opportunity for connection and real conversation. When someone asks this question, they might want to know what you do for a living, where you're from, or any number of biographical details. But the very root is this: What makes you unique? Of course there are at least a thousand ways you're exceptional, but you've got to be concise. The solution is to create your own Signature Story.

What is your Signature Story? It is the "story" you will use in a variety of

Career Confession

WHERE DO I START?

It's the question that haunts me. Whether it's at a new friend's BBQ, on a first date, or in an interview, the question sits, lurking, waiting to be asked. I brace myself as it glides past the lips of the interrogator.

Why don't you tell me a bit about yourself?

My mind races with my own series of questions: *Where do I start? What does he really want to know? Where is the balance between boring him to tears and luring him into deeper conversation with a scintillating tidbit? Why do people ask this frickin' question? How in the world do I describe my whole self in a couple sentences?*

I then proceed to promise myself (again) that I won't get caught in this situation next time. I will craft an answer. I will find a way. I will write it down. I will practice it in front of a mirror.

My confession: I won't do any of the above. I will get caught in the same situation again and again. I simply don't know how to answer the question.

Isabella, graphic artist

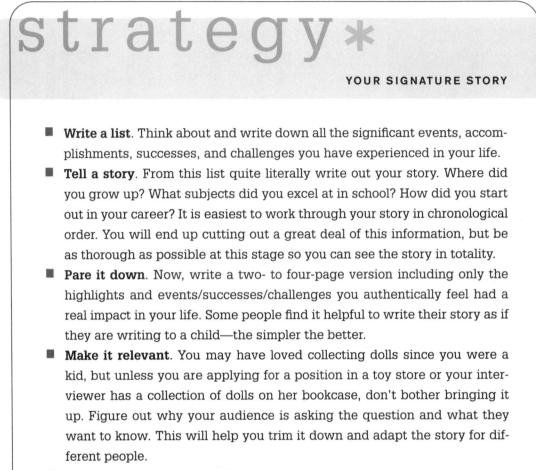

strategy*

YOUR SIGNATURE STORY

- **Write a list**. Think about and write down all the significant events, accomplishments, successes, and challenges you have experienced in your life.
- **Tell a story**. From this list quite literally write out your story. Where did you grow up? What subjects did you excel at in school? How did you start out in your career? It is easiest to work through your story in chronological order. You will end up cutting out a great deal of this information, but be as thorough as possible at this stage so you can see the story in totality.
- **Pare it down**. Now, write a two- to four-page version including only the highlights and events/successes/challenges you authentically feel had a real impact in your life. Some people find it helpful to write their story as if they are writing to a child—the simpler the better.
- **Make it relevant**. You may have loved collecting dolls since you were a kid, but unless you are applying for a position in a toy store or your interviewer has a collection of dolls on her bookcase, don't bother bringing it up. Figure out why your audience is asking the question and what they want to know. This will help you trim it down and adapt the story for different people.
- **Paint a visual picture with your words**. Create an engaging story your audience will feel a part of. Use descriptive words and phrases.

different lengths and formats to explain to others Who You Think You Are. This is the story I wish I had ready the night of the charity event when I was asked the critical question. Your story is unique to you, and depending upon your audience and the length of time you have available, you will make changes as you go. I've struggled with my own Story over the years, especially since I created a career building business. Experience has taught me that it's helpful to have not just one, but a full repertoire of stories to draw from.

When you're selecting your Signature Story, there's one critical thing to remember: Your Signature Story is as much about what your audience wants to know as it is about what you want to tell them. Take the time to ask questions and assess the situation, and pull out the most relevant version for your "audience."

PART TWO
PROJECT A PROFESSIONAL IMAGE

Feeling confident in your professional image gives you incredible power. You walk with infinitely more strut than slouch, and you're ready to tackle whatever challenges come your way. You feel "right," and it shows. In this section, I'll discuss how you can use both your professional look and your communication skills to express yourself with style—and with substance.

Dress For Success

Clothing, just like your work, is an expression of Who You Think You Are, not a definition. Designer labels alone don't make you stylish or mark you as a professional. Personal style has two key elements: It's situation- or job-appropriate, and it reflects the best of who you are. You feel perfectly dressed and ready to kick ass—all at the same time. What's appropriate will also depend on your industry. An investment banker can't arrive at work in shorts, just as a camp counselor can't be decked out in silk and tweed. The truth is, your colleagues, clients, and bosses all make assumptions based on your appearance. Take charge of your look and reap the benefits.

Career Confession

THE PONCHO

I've been slipping at work. Not in terms of my actual work or my relationships with my colleagues . . . I've been slipping in style. My suits are boring, and they don't make me feel cute—and every time I go shopping for new ones, I come home empty-handed (nice petite suits are hard to find!).

But last week I crossed the line. I reached deep into my inner-corporate-rebel and even deeper into my closet to exhume the one article of clothing that could possibly get me through the day: the poncho. Not the wildly colored "rough" kind, this one was a bit sophisticated—I bought it, after all. I walked out the door with my hair swept up (too emotionally drained to wash it), pearl earrings in place (attempt to include one chic item in outfit), a snug cap-sleeve tee (last clean shirt left), and the glorious gray knit poncho to cover it up. It was all wrong, and I knew it.

As soon as I arrived at work, my closest male colleague told me I looked like a mushroom. He even convinced me to tuck in my arms, crouch on the floor, and pull the poncho over my feet. At that very moment, a top managing director walked past and shot me a withering glance. Not cool.

Sophia, software developer

First Impressions

The twentieth interview of the day and I'd wager I've seen more cleavage than a Beverly Hills plastic surgeon. Part of me desperately wanted to suggest to the last potential candidate that she'd have a better chance finding a job at Hooters than she would at this company. If there is one piece of advice I could offer any-

---

One-on-One

The Perfect Outfit
It's a suit or skirt or blouse or pair of trousers that you almost forget you're wearing. It doesn't itch or ride up your ass when you are sitting down. The perfect outfit makes you feel at once comfortable and comforted.

---

one beginning their career Quest, it would be this: Learn a little about the company you are applying to and dress appropriately. It's not that your talent, experience, and abilities are not critical, but please don't underestimate the importance and impact of professional image. It's the first impression you give to your potential employer, client, and colleagues.

Although the saying is "never judge a book by its cover," the fact remains that when presented with hundreds of applicants for particular positions, that is exactly what people do. Fairly or unfairly, people sense that the effort and attention to detail you put into presenting yourself has a direct relationship to the effort and attention you will put into your work.

Here's another pointer I could have used back in my miniskirt days:

Sexy, risqué, provocative—it's all in the eye of the beholder. What you think is sexy someone else might describe as downright slutty. Although you might feel confident and attractive in your sexy clothes, others might be uncomfortable with

> **Beauty, to me, is about being comfortable in your own skin. That, or a kick-ass red lipstick.**
> —Gwyneth Paltrow

your wardrobe. Provocative clothing will not prevent career success—think Erin Brockovich in her micro-miniskirts and low-cut tops. It might, however, distract your co-workers, boss, or clients away from your most powerful asset—your mind. Here are some tips if you're opting to reveal some skin:

strategy *

If you're building your first professional wardrobe or are simply looking to update your style, here are a few pointers. Although this strategy is skewed toward a corporate workplace, it's a basic collection that can be dressed up or down and given a more creative, funky spin, if necessary.

Open the doors of your closet. What have you got? Pull out all the clothes you no longer wear, that you don't fit in to, or that are obviously outdated. Put them in a pile for donation (this is often fun to do with a friend), and make an inventory of what you have left. The following are just a few of the work-wear essentials. Use this to assess what you have and what you need:

Great pair of shoes Start with black and expand from there. Consider your comfort level. High heels look elegant with both pants and skirts, but remember, nothing's worse than teetering in pain as you struggle to keep up with your colleagues.

Elegant suit If you are purchasing your first suit, I can offer three hints.

- Make circumstance- and event-appropriate choices. There is a difference between the Friday afternoon staff meeting over drinks and the Monday morning appointment with clients.

- Balance a sexy piece of clothing with a more traditional item. For example, wear a risqué blouse with a more conservative suit.

- You can create the image of sex appeal without being overt. An open-toe shoe with red toenail polish is perfect.

1) Choose a color that goes with everything—black or dark gray is perfect and doesn't require frequent dry-cleaning. 2) It's worth investing in a good-quality suit. 3) Look for a suit with a matching skirt and pants to increase its versatility.

White blouse These come in all shapes and sizes. Use your blouses and shirts to mix up your look.

Purse/briefcase Look for a workbag or briefcase that can hold a small purse. Too many bags can be cumbersome.

Outerwear jacket Whether you live in Florida or New York, choose a weather-appropriate jacket. You'll likely wear your jacket every day during the winter months, so choose something that works with as many outfits as possible and can handle the wear and tear.

Ensure everything you already own is in good condition, dry-cleaned, and polished. If you're going shopping for some missing items and you're not sure what you like, flip through magazines and observe the people around you. What styles do you admire on others? And don't forget to check out vintage and secondhand stores. Even if you're on a budget, you will often find some amazing, one-of-a-kind buys to liven up your professional wardrobe.

Get The Word Out

In an elevator, at a networking event, on your resumé, at a morning meeting— you have myriad opportunities to differentiate yourself with your professional yet unique style of communication. Your ability to communicate will create the opportunities to break away from the pack. This section is dedicated to the simple

> **The one fashion truth I know is this: You have to dress to please yourself.**
> —Beyoncé Knowles

yet often overlooked elements of successful communication. Here are a few communication tips, topics, and tidbits to consider:

Questions

Colleges should offer a course titled, "Getting Beyond How Are You?" Your ability to ask engaging questions and elicit personal information will help you create lasting relationships, understand others' needs, and, most important, help people feel you are interested in their lives and their feelings. Here's the thing: Everyone loves the opportunity to answer questions and talk about themselves.

It's only through listening that you learn, and I never want to stop learning.

—Drew Barrymore

The good stuff exists past the first level of the conversation, and questions are the surefire way to get you there. Here are some questions and sentence starters that will help you get to that next level of communication:

- What did you learn from that experience?

- What advice would you give to someone in the same situation?

- What were some of the funny things that happened during that time?

- What surprised you?

- What did you learn about yourself through that experience?

- Give me an example.

Written Communication

It still surprises me. I will receive an e-mail from someone asking whether we are hiring, and the message is littered with spelling and grammar errors. Even the most basic stuff—their/there, too/to—it happens often enough to make it worth mentioning. Spell check every single document that leaves your desk. Have someone else proofread important e-mails, or save them and read them the next day. Be succinct. If you have difficultly articulating yourself in writing, dictate your message into a handheld recorder and then compose on paper. Invest in a business-writing course if you need it—and even if you don't.

> ## One-on-One
>
> ### *Over the Top*
> There is an expression that suggests, "Your greatest strength is often your greatest weakness." When it comes to the world of work, being passionate and enthusiastic are wonderful qualities. The danger, however, is going over the top. Be passionate; be enthusiastic; but be aware. Your energy has the potential to excite and intrigue people, but also to scare and turn people off. In the world of work, you must be constantly aware of your audience. Gauge their interest and their demeanor, and tailor your approach and expressions to ensure they listen to every valuable word you have to say.

Swearing

I love integrating a choice swear word into a passionate personal or professional discussion, but opting to swear is a risk, and my recommendation is to err on the side of caution.

Swearing protocol largely depends on your work environment. I worked in one office where every Monday the boss would yell out her open office door, "Where the f$*&k is the latest sales report?" Swearing also depends on what comes naturally. I've seen powerful, intelligent leaders who poignantly punctuate a presentation with a swear word, and I've seen others for whom swearing fits like an ill-fitting pair of leather pants. It's not necessarily the word that's offensive, it's the style with which you use it. And as a young woman beginning your Quest, you'll need to exercise added caution here—you can't afford to be seen as less than professional.

Gossiping

There is something exciting about getting the dirt, but one of the best pieces of advice I ever received was to stay away from office gossip. You might believe that sharing a piece of gossip will gain you favor with your colleagues; you will be considered important having access to the inside scoop. The truth? You will be seen as a busybody—a person who cannot be trusted, someone not to be taken seriously, and, most important, someone who has too much time on her hands.

There is never a right time or a good reason to gossip. Gossip is hurtful, destructive, dangerous, often misinformed, and makes those involved look like they are better suited to the playground than the workplace. Take yourself, your career, and your colleagues seriously. Do not get pulled into the game of show-and-tell.

Body Language

Naturally enthusiastic, I wave my hands passionately (and sometimes violently) in the air to supplement my verbal message. After an especially important business meeting, my mentor and boss dropped me a helpful note.

> *To: Nicole*
> *From: Janet*
> *Re: Taking flight*
> *Love your enthusiasm. Don't love watching you talk with your hands with such vigor. I'm afraid you will take flight and leave me to attend to the meeting alone.*

> **I keep waiting to meet a man who has more balls than I do.**
> —Salma Hayek

Posture, the pace and firmness of your walk, eye contact, hand gestures, hair fiddling, nail picking—these are all forms of nonverbal communication we don't always consciously think about. Ask someone you trust to watch the ways in which you might subconsciously be distracting your listener.

Self-Promotion

It might feel arrogant to say "I am smart; I am talented; I am the best in my field," but the reality is, it's not—especially when you are prepared to substanti-

---

✳ One-on-One

Over Promotion

I once worked with a woman who would tell anyone who would listen how outstanding her skills were and how desirable she was to other potential employers. At first I thought, this is great—someone who is willing to promote herself! But after weeks of all talk and no action, her self-aggrandizing speeches grew tired.

On one fateful afternoon, the company CEO stopped by to have a visit with the staff. Predictably, this woman—let's call her Anita—launched into her now-routine stories of grandiosity with her new prey. I watched the CEO's face turn from impressed, to bored, to downright agitated. Finally, Anita lamented the fact that a headhunter had just called and wanted to know if she was looking for a new opportunity.

The CEO, seemingly trying to restrain himself, finally said. "Well, I'd suggest you call the headhunter back and let him know you're on the market."

---

ate your statement with action. Think of it this way: A Wildly Sophisticated self-promoter is someone who has the power to make a bold statement and the courage to follow up with even bolder action.

The rules of stylish self-promotion:

- Focus on the truth.

- Talk about your success through experience.

- Follow up with action.

Career Confession

GUT FEELING

I'm going to be sick. What a complete disaster. I knew better than to ignore my gut on this one. I just got off the phone with one of the country's top broadcasting companies, and I killed one of the most important negotiations of my career. My boss was pulling the strings, and I was basically her spokesperson (although I felt more like a puppet).

The global sponsorship deal was all but sealed when my boss decided to see if we could get even more money. She instructed me to go above the person I was working with (obviously a bad idea) and call a high-level CEO to play our trump card. Yikes. I advised my boss against it. Would we really want to make our contact look bad? My boss assured me it would be interesting to push the company further and see what we could get. My stomach hurt. I knew in my gut this was the wrong way to negotiate, but I felt caught between my boss and my instincts.

Well, you guessed it. The deal is off, and now it's my job to clean up the mess with my contact—a woman whose reputation I seriously tarnished. My lesson: When you know the right thing to do, do it. If not, you'll suffer the consequences—especially if it's your name attached to the fallout.

Joanne, marketing executive

PART THREE
FIGURE OUT WHAT YOU STAND FOR

As we begin to better understand ourselves—defining our values, expectations, and dreams—we have a responsibility to act on that knowledge.

Self-expression doesn't end with a Prada blouse or a perfectly articulated argument. Image counts, yes, but once you're past high school, people start watching your actions. What do you stand for? Do you walk your own talk?

The commitment to honor your own vision takes integrity—a refusal to compromise your talents and your inner sense of self. But expressing your integrity takes courage. The first person you must be accountable to is you, but personal accountability doesn't stop inside your head. Decide what you stand for and use your ambitions, boundaries, and choices to bring your values to life. As you begin to define and understand yourself, it becomes increasingly difficult to cross your own boundaries.

In today's world of work, you don't have to be hired by the Soprano family to be asked to do something you're not quite comfortable with (let alone something illegal). In the face of a request to fib to a client or fudge the numbers, ask yourself this: *Would I be ashamed to share the truth of the situation with my best friend, parents, or partner?* If you answer yes, if you feel that you would have to lie in order to save face with those you love, get out—fast.

Principled Ambition

Many young women I meet say they're conflicted about ambition and ethics. Maybe it's the images: From film to fiction to real-life headlines, we see successful and supposedly self-sufficient businessmen and -women who have eagerly crushed toes (and more) on their climb up the ladder. Sure, the business world might not have a stellar reputation for fair and ethical practices. But as you know, reputations are not necessarily reality. We're far more likely to hear about sweatshop labor and "creative" accounting practices than the thousands of responsible, ethical organizations out there. It's often the proverbial bad seed spoiling the whole bunch.

It comes down to this: you have to trust your

> The old views of business as a jungle where only the vicious survive will, I hope, soon be giving way to a new view of business as a community where only the responsible will lead.
> —Anita Roddick

strategy*

- **Redefine ambition.** Ambition is, by definition, "an eager or strong desire to achieve something such as fame or power." Ambition is about desire; it is about discipline; it is about going after what you want; but it is *not* about moving forward at the expense of others. Decide to take back the word or use another, but whatever you do, don't feel ashamed of your desire to advance and excel.

- **Lead by example.** You don't have to start your own business to instill a higher level of integrity and moral standard within your workplace. In my experience most people don't start or intend to act unethically, but in many cases, they believe there's no other way out. If you feel a colleague or boss is misguided or is following an unethical road, think through some alternate solutions and bring them forward. If he or she decides to continue along the unethical path, actively pursue another—lead by example.

- **Get over yourself.** If you want to create success and are searching for the desire to fuel your ambitions, attach your career to serving others and making a contribution to the world. Is there a way you can connect your drive and success with helping others? Mentor, donate a portion of your earnings to a cause you believe in, or be a Big Sister. The options are endless.

- **Be prepared to walk away.** If you encounter a business practice that makes you uncomfortable—something you know in your heart is not quite right—be prepared to walk away. I truly believe that by lowering your standards and working in a capacity that is not consistent with your values and sense of integrity, beyond acting unethically and hurting others, you are hurting yourself. It's not always easy to stand up to the dominant opinion or workplace culture, but in the end, it's even harder to compromise yourself.

own power and ethical guidelines. If your workplace encourages back-stabbing, manipulative, or simply unacceptable tactics for achieving "success," it's time to speak up or move on. And whether you're managing your career or starting a business of your own, create your own rules! Build a business—and a career—that you believe in. Can you get ahead and still uphold your own values? Yes, yes, and yes again. Trust that your ethics and ambition can not only coexist, but that this powerful combination will actually help you succeed.

Draw Your Boundaries

Do you recognize this person? Within minutes of meeting your new co-worker you know her boyfriend just dumped her, her mom is pre-menopausal, and she hasn't slept in days thanks to a killer migraine. If this woman is anything like the people I've known, it won't be long before she's calling you "sweetie" and embracing you in a big, fat hug.

> The most important lesson I've learned in this business is how to say no. I have said no to a lot of temptations, and I am glad I did.
> —Penelope Cruz

If there's one thing I can promise you, it's this: Your ability to create boundaries is one of the hands-down most memorable, effective ways to differentiate and express yourself. Be aware of where your personal boundaries stop and your professional boundaries begin.

These are just a few of the confusing and challenging boundary issues I most frequently encounter with clients. Do any of these quotes sound familiar?

"I didn't mean to make out with my boss at the office party."
The line is crossed. You can think about your boundaries until your head throbs, but it's pointless to live in fear of stepping over the line. Why? You'll truly understand your limits when you cross them. You don't even have to spend

Career Confession

THE CONVERSATION

I work with someone who, although a nice enough man, feels the need to speak in condescending tones and refers to everything we do as a team as his own work. Over the two years I have worked with this man, I have just smiled, ignored him, and gone home to vent and complain to my friends and family. Finally, one of my closest friends told me she was tired of hearing me complain about him. "If you don't like how he speaks to you, let him know . . . and if you're not willing to do that, quit bitching about it." To the point and very true.

So I made up my mind to have "the conversation." I mean, what's worse—facing the fear of having a difficult conversation or spending the next year suffering in silence?

I prepared my notes and made my points. I focused on his positive attributes as well as the things that would make me more receptive to him. I won't lie and say it was easy—it wasn't. I can tell you, however, that now he's making an honest effort to change his tone and be inclusive.

Jane, public relations manager

time thinking about it. Your body will send immediate signals when you've crossed the line, and it's up to you to protect yourself.

Even if you do step over your boundaries, you're free to come back. The experience will actually help you draw better limits next time. And don't think a "line cross" ever defines you. So you made out with your boss. You're not going to do it again, and you're definitely not doomed to a life of professional prostitution.

> **The problem is not that you attract unavailable people—the problem is that you give them your number.**
> —Marianne Williamson

Career Confession

IT'S MY LIFE

In high school, we were scheduled to take a special career inventory test on the computer. This was before the Internet or CD-ROMs emerged, so my teacher raved about this "revolutionary" software program. All we had to do was answer a series of multiple choice questions based on our personalities, skills, interests, and work styles. Then *voilà!* The program would select our ideal career. *Finally! I'll find some answers,* I thought.

I dutifully responded to all the questions, struggling to be as honest as possible.

"Do you enjoy working with your hands?"

Absolutely, I thought, and clicked "yes." I continued through the questions and held my breath as the computer narrowed the thousands of careers down to my one perfect job.

I squinted in disbelief as I read the answer: mortician.

Now, no offense if this is your chosen profession. Every career can be fabulous and challenging. But I had always thought of myself as creative, inventive, and energetic, and I loved being around people— living, breathing people.

That day not only made a great story, but it taught me a valuable lesson: It's all up to me. Besides, would I really want to live someone else's vision for my life? I shut down my computer and answered a resounding "no."

Allison, journalist

strategy *

When you're drawing and defining your boundaries, you'll eventually be faced with some hard conversations. They're never fun, but they're always empowering. Here are the key points to remember when you're facing a tough discussion:

■ **Get it over with.** Just like any challenging task, be careful you don't prolong your conversation and your agony. In most instances, wishing the conflict or situation will go away is not enough—you will have to face it. Waiting to have the conversation is worse than just bucking up and getting the job done.

■ **Define the real issue.** Clearly articulate your reason for the meeting. You don't like the way your boss takes responsibility for your work. There is simply too little support in the office. Before the meeting, be honest with yourself about the true reason for the conversation. Have you ever noticed

Have patience with everything unresolved in your heart and try to love the questions themselves as if they were locked rooms or books written in a very foreign language. Live the questions now.
—Rainer Maria Rilke

"I'm not going to tell him to back off; I want him to like me."
Work is not a popularity contest. The "him" in this scenario is a young woman's boss, and in one form or another, I hear this sentiment way too often. Please repeat after me: Work is not a popularity contest. There is an immense difference between being liked and being respected. People respect others who respect themselves enough to establish personal and professional boundaries—people who have opinions, people who demand what they're worth, people who say no.

how when you're fighting with your boyfriend, it looks and sounds like you're arguing over the remote, when in fact there is something much more menacing below the surface? The same logic applies at work.

■ **Set an agenda.** There's nothing worse than leaving the conversation only to have to go and say "Oh yeah, and I forgot . . ." Conversely, there's the risk of going too far, of saying more than you are prepared for in the heat of the conversation. Spend some time writing down exactly what you want to cover. Remember, it's difficult to take back your words.

■ **Determine your desired outcome and solution.** What do you want the outcome of the conversation to be? In some instances, you will work through a solution together; in others, you will be responsible for coming up with your own solution. There is danger in having a conversation—telling your co-worker you don't like her propensity to use racist jokes—and the person doesn't respect you enough to change their behavior. You want to be sure you have a measure or outcome to assess how the situation has changed and improved.

"I swear she picks on me."
Call your bully's bluff. Bullies can sniff out fear a mile away. They sense your vulnerability, get poised to attack, and rely on the fact that you won't call them on their actions. Just like in the schoolyard, bullying is rooted in insecurity—*theirs,* not yours. I can almost promise that if you call your bully's bluff and expressly define your unwillingness to take her bullshit, she will back off and find a new victim.

"I'm so stupid. I can't believe I told her I forgot the deadline."
People will believe you. What are you telling people about yourself? You might be surprised. Although it's crucial to define what others can say and do

to you, don't forget about what you're revealing to others. Monitor your conversations. What do you tell people about yourself? People will believe what you tell them, so refrain from saying, "I'm so lazy" or "I'm so stupid." Tell them you are smart, and they will believe you. If you tell people you're tired and lack focus, they will believe you, and even worse, *you* will believe you.

"I thought we really made a great connection, but she didn't say hi on the way to her office."
Your boss is not your friend. You will make amazing friendships in the workplace—maybe even with your boss—but please remember, unlike in mutual, healthy friendships, there is a definitive power imbalance within a reporting relationship. It's your boss writing up your performance review, signing your paychecks, and assigning your projects—not your friend. If you do find yourself with a budding friendship at work, take the time to acknowledge and define the boundaries between your personal and professional relationships.

Walk Through Life

One of the most difficult parts of the Quest is the anxiety, the deep-seated urgency to pick the right path, and the desire to know today what comes next. Thanks to generations of courageous women, we have more options than ever before, and with that freedom comes a sense of responsibility. We not only feel pressure to choose, but we worry that our choices have to be perfect. We want to gaze into a crystal ball and avoid the messy process of living through the questions. Sometimes the sheer volume of possible choices is overwhelming—immobilizing.

> I want to walk through life instead of being dragged through it.
> —Alanis Morissette

I'm here to tell you to forget the crystal ball. You don't need it. Forget about finding the perfect answers, and focus on yourself. The solutions and answers lie at the heart of Who You Think You Are.

strategy*

OVERWHELMED BY THE OPTIONS

Choice is a wonderful thing, but sometimes the options can become over-whelming—especially if you have many interests. Work that challenges and excites you needs to come from your core. It flows from Who You Think You Are. Sometimes you have to think dramatically to get to the heart of your passions. Ask yourself:

- If you won the lottery or were independently wealthy, what would you do with your time? What would your days be like?
- If you were to "start over" with no pressures or expectations from friends, family, partners, etc., what would you do? How would you live?
- If all work was equally paid and held the same social status, what would you want to do?
- What would you regret not doing if you only had months left to live?

When you begin to express yourself by making authentic, natural choices, your path appears with each step. You simply begin to walk through life. The decisions become infinitely easier, and you begin to gain momentum. And here's the best news: Your Quest does not require one monumental choice. The way you decide to live your Quest every single day is your choice. You will move naturally toward success when you follow your genuine desires and instincts.

❄   ❄   ❄

Well, I made it through the "dress code" talk. Thank God my boss didn't overtly point to me (and my too-short skirt) in front of all my colleagues. Who's kidding who?—she didn't have to.

The next day, I arrived in a very appropriate pair of pinstripe pants, and you know what? I felt infinitely better. I knew I was well dressed and I wasn't going to face another embarrassing meeting. I could leave it all behind and focus on my work. My miniskirts were great for college and even a little advantageous for my part-time job as a restaurant hostess, but they didn't cut it at the office.

What I've come to understand since that embarrassing memo is this: Taking charge of your personal image isn't frivolous or manipulative. It's smart. It's simply a matter of capitalizing on what and who you already are. In fact, the more authentically you express yourself—in your dress, your speech, and your personal dealings with others—the more naturally captivating you will be.

4

Are You Up for a Challenge?

Taking Risks

"Nicole, can you come in here for a minute?" I jumped, startled by the volume coming through the intercom.

I walked into my boss's office to find her on the phone. With a moment to concentrate, I studied the wall behind her desk. Who's Who, Entrepreneur of the Year, MBA, Ph.D.—clearly, too much time on her hands. As an ambitious twenty-eight-year-old consultant, I made a Note to Self: Find a colleague who I can bribe to nominate me for something—anything—that will produce a piece of paper I can frame.

"Yes, as I explained to your secretary, I will be in the Philippines on the date of the conference. I will be sending a senior consultant from my firm to make the presentation. Her name is Nicole Williams." My ears perked up.

"She will contact you later this afternoon." Eyebrow arched with intrigue, I took a seat as she hung up the phone.

"I've volunteered you to present at the World Services Congress in Atlanta," she said with a sly smile. "Maria booked your flight. I've written some notes for the presentation, and the delegate list is in this file."

I reached across her desk. Before she let go of the file she looked me square in the eye and asked, "Are you up for a challenge?"

Are You Up for a Challenge? is the question that makes our heart beat a little faster and brings out the fight in us. As I headed back to my office, I started to flip through the delegate list, curious about what this mysterious challenge entailed. I stopped dead in my tracks. The list of attendees was a veritable Who's Who of the business world—everyone from the CEO of Viacom to the vice president of the United States—all of whom would be expecting *me* to give a killer presentation.

I'd like to tell you I was excited, thrilled, delighted to be asked, but I wasn't. I was scared shitless. It was time for emergency measures. Within the hour I was sitting in the local Starbucks sipping coffee and asking my best friend Jenn for help, direction, solace—anything that would make this challenge feel a little more comfortable.

The consummate risk-taker and professional rebel, Jenn suggests, "Say no. If the risk is too much for you, just tell her thanks, but no thanks." There's nothing like a little "maybe you can't," to both simultaneously elate and compel me to step up to the plate. As frightened as I was, I knew this was my next step on my Quest. Walking back into the office, I looked longingly at the woman running the mail through the postage meter. In my head I wished it could be easier, but in my heart I knew it couldn't be.

Here's the deal. The Quest for Success is filled with challenge. Risk is inherent in the creation of a career that demands the Wildly Sophisticated elements of self-promotion, action, and excellence. Fears of the unknown, vulnerability, and failure are the greatest stumbling blocks we all have to grapple with as we build our careers.

But risk is a part of life. It's at the heart of learning, growing, and breakthrough experiences. When we embrace calculated risks, we stretch the limits of what we thought we could do. Even when we risk and lose, there's still value in the experience. In fact, taking a risk and *losing* is one of the best ways to improve.

As a young woman launching your career, so much of what you are challenged by and are experiencing is new. And newness is a direct path to fear! The goal of this chapter is to explore fear on your own terms, to look it in the face, to own it—in order to get through it.

Fear is highly personal. What makes you scared, what looks like risk to you, will not look like risk to your best friend, parents, or boyfriend. I can promise that although your desire to risk and the accompanying sense of fear isn't going to go away, there are ways to more fully embrace and harness the energy of fear. That is what this chapter is all about. There is a responsibility in having big dreams, and yes, the potential for failure increases in direct proportion to your risks. You have to ask yourself the questions: *What am I willing to dream? What am I willing to risk?* Embracing risk, examining our fears, committing to excellence—these are scary prospects.

Are You Up for a Challenge?

In the first part of this chapter, I'll talk about taking risks, building confidence, and when to take leaps. In part two, I'll look at facing your fears and living with the discomfort that comes from stretching your limits.

PART ONE
MAKING THE LEAP

My friend Kelly is an inspiration—a daredevil kind of inspiration. Every birthday Kel commits to doing something she is afraid of. As her birthday approaches, I'm always a bit curious to learn what's on the agenda. A few years ago, I was mortified to learn Kel's challenge included a ferry ride, a two-hour drive, a bridge, some stretchy rope, and a wild, racing river below it—the bungee jump. Always looking to live vicariously through Kelly, I agreed to be the designated driver.

I thought I was just there for moral support . . . so how did I end up on the edge of a bridge, hundreds of feet in the air, with a harness around my ankles? Something inside told me this was a risk I *needed* to take.

Kel allowed me to go first, and as I stood on the ledge, I remember actually having to will my body to lean forward far enough to free-fall off the plank. While this was quite literally a leap, everything I've needed to know about embracing challenge and risk—about taking the leap—I learned on that fateful day.

Timing

Once I had actually made the decision to jump, I discovered the truth behind the expression "timing is everything." There is a very fine and precarious line between taking the time to assess if your leap is worth taking and waiting so long you miss the opportunity . . . or you scare yourself into a tizzy. The reality is, I begged Kelly to let me go first. I was willing to take the risk, I understood the potential for danger, but I didn't want to spend any more time than I had to dwelling on the vision of the snapped bungee cord. In the face of risk and challenge, timing is crucial.

> **Sometimes if you wait too long, the chances just go away.**
> —Sarah Michelle Gellar

When to Take a Risk

Accepting a challenge, reaching beyond what's comfortable, risking—these are all amazing parts of life, regardless of your age. But as a young woman, you are at a unique time in your life that makes taking a leap now a great and potentially less-risky investment.

One of the things I consistently hear from women in their 40s—most of them with partners, newborn kids, and mortgages—is that they wish they had taken more risks as they were initially building their career. This is the perfect time to take a chance. You likely have less responsibility now than you will at any other point in your life. The even better news is that if you flop, all is not lost. You have tons of time to regain your footing. You will have tremendous learning to apply to all the other risks to come in your future. And let's be honest—as a less-experienced professional, your mistakes will be forgiven and forgotten more quickly.

When NOT to Take a Risk

Knowing when to risk and when NOT to risk is a critical part of creating success. In today's driving world of work, where pushing your boundaries in the face of risk is the name of the game, it is tremendously brave to say no—to wait, to have patience, and to acknowledge it's simply not the right time. How do you know when it's time to step away? Here are a few guidelines:

- **You're frazzled and exhausted.** This is not the same as feeling tired. There will be many times when you don't want to get up early to finish a presentation or quadruple-check the fifty-page grant application. In these cases, you do have the energy—it's just a matter of digging deeper to access it. When you've actually drained your emotional and physical reserves, it's time to go easy and build yourself up again.

- **You're trying to please someone else.** Or maybe you don't even know why you're doing it. Taking a chance requires your full commitment. You can only succeed if you know what's at stake, why you want to push yourself, and what the potential payoff will be.

- **You're not prepared.** Even if you've taken every possible step to swing the odds in your favor, you might still feel nervous. That's good. It means you're emotionally invested, and you can harness those nerves to achieve your peak performance. But if you're genuinely not ready—and only you can know what that will look and feel like—you're heading for a crash.

- **You don't have the support you need.** Are your friends and family behind you? Or if they're not, do you feel strong enough to move forward on your own? From financial stability to scheduling issues, support comes in many forms. Ensure you have the right backup in place.

Intuition

Not only did I have a feeling I would live through the bungee jump, I had an even greater sense that if I didn't take the leap I would look back and regret the

> **Intuition is knowing without knowing why.**
> —Gavin De Becker, *The Gift of Fear*

decision. As afraid as I was, in my gut I knew I was not only going to survive but flourish in taking the leap. There is a dynamic and uncertain balance where risk is concerned. On one hand, we can't simply disregard fear and distress—these feelings indicate danger. On the other hand, in the face of the unknown, fear is a reality. It is your gut, your sense of instinct that will guide you in the face of risk.

Intuition, a sixth sense—call it what you want. If you are struggling to know if you are truly ready to take your next leap, there are two things you need—patience and quiet. In the face of major decisions, take the time to shut out the voices in your head and listen to your heart. It's not that you won't feel fear; you will. What you are looking for is a sense of calm or certainty underneath the fear that although difficult to describe, is undeniably present.

Breathe

No one actually believes this, but I took breathing lessons and I have the receipt to prove it. One day, I'm sitting in the office with a colleague and she asks me, "Are you breathing?" Breaking my concentration to look over at her, I respond a bit perturbed, "Of course I'm still breathing—why do you ask?"

Have you ever consciously thought about the way you breathe? Well, I have the best news for you. This might sound a little New Age-y, but breathing is the key to finding your instinct. If you have ever sat frustrated, tapping your fingers, waiting for your "answer" to suddenly appear, don't hold your breath—literally, don't hold your breath.

Courage

It requires courage to leap, to let go of what you've known and grab hold of what you have only dreamt will be there. I assumed from the business license on the wall that others had jumped and survived, but in the face of danger there is always the "what if?" What if the rope breaks? What if my feet slip out of the holders? What if the operator had a few too many last night and forgets how to operate the lift? Courage is born when you can feel, see, hear, and taste the fear and you make the decision to leap anyway. The magic begins when you courageously leave what you've known to trust and hope for something more.

> Your attitude to me, says the breath, is your attitude to life. Welcome me . . . Embrace me fully. Let me nourish you completely, then set me free. Move with me, dance with me, sing with me, sigh with me . . . love me, trust me, don't try to control me.
>
> —Long Chen Pa

One of the bravest career moves I've ever witnessed didn't involve a multi-million-dollar deal or a solo show on Broadway. It was a quiet but dazzling feat of self-determination and personal strength.

Elaine was on a career path that, from the outside, looked enviably clear. Her family is one of those household names in the neighborhood. Her father is a surgeon; her mother, a psychiatrist; and her older brother? A radiologist. Elaine worked straight through high school to university to medical school. No one pushed her into medicine exactly, but everyone assumed she'd follow her family's lead.

Just as she was beginning her residency, Elaine came down with a bronchial infection that totally laid her out. She had to take a week off (something totally unheard of in her whirlwind life), and she found herself camped out on the couch watching daytime TV. Somewhere between *Days of Our Lives* and *Oprah,*

> Sometimes you just have to take the leap and build your wings on the way down.
>
> —Kobi Yamada

Elaine finally acknowledged a little voice whispering in her ear. What comes next was the hottest piece of news to hit her circle of friends in years. Elaine quit school.

Her parents were horrified, all the neighbors whispered when she walked by, and her classmates thought she had suffered a nervous breakdown. But even after an enormous investment of time and some major money, Elaine had the courage to step away. Superficially, medicine was the easier route. It was all set out in front of her—the connections, the process, and (who's kidding who) the money. Anything else would be fuzzy and uncertain. Still, she trusted her instincts and believed that with time, nothing would be easier than following her heart. Three years later, she's a high-profile pastry chef and she isn't looking back.

Confidence

In the face of the bungee jump, I called upon every single experience of risk in my memory bank to give me the confidence I needed to leap. On a physical level, jumping from a bridge is a far cry from what I do in my career. But strangely enough, it is that day I think of most often when I'm on the verge of taking a risk in my work. In the face of risk, confidence fills you with a sense of certainty, a feeling that, "No matter what, I'm going to be alright." The great news is that confidence can be nourished and grown. Understanding the following Wildly Sophisticated Rules of Confidence can help you develop a greater sense of self-assurance.

The Wildly Sophisticated Rules of Confidence

- **No one can give it to you.** I'm reminded of a boyfriend who had everything going for him—good looks, strong mind, hard body—everything but confidence. Confidence does not emerge from a magic number on

strategy*

Courage is not exclusive to Lance Armstrong, Christopher Reeve, Anita Hill, or Christianne Amanpour. Courageousness might feel like one of those things we don't feel worthy of identifying within ourselves, but I can promise that you are, and have been, brave. I love in the story of *The Wizard of Oz* when the Cowardly Lion asks Oz for his courage. Oz responds back, "True courage is in facing danger when you are afraid, and that you have in plenty."

As I talked about in the introduction, risk is a very personal thing. This strategy asks you not to compare your courage to anyone else, but to think about all the times you've been afraid and have decided to leap anyway. The goal is to remember your experience of bravery so you can access that courage when you need it most.

- **Brainstorm a list of all the leaps you have taken in your life.** Take the time to write down each and every experience you've had that has pushed your limits and required courage.
- **Remember in detail the actual leap.** Think about the exact point where you left what you knew with a sense of trust and faith to experience something more or different. Leaping is the space between what you've known and what you are about to know. What did the leap feel like? Describe it in as much detail as possible.
- **Visualize your next leap.** Envision the actual process. You're walking to the podium to give a speech: how do you feel, how do you handle your feelings, and how does the experience play out from beginning to a successful end? Imagine smiling and presenting yourself with clarity and confidence. Hear the audience laugh at your jokes. Bask in the applause, and enjoy the satisfaction of overcoming your jitters to accomplish something great.

the scale or from the compliments of others. Confidence comes through you and you alone. No one can give it to you.

> One isn't necessarily born with courage, but one is born with potential. Without courage, We cannot practice any other virtue with consistency. We can't be kind, true, merciful, generous, or honest.
>
> —Maya Angelou

- **Fake it till you make it (confidence, not skills).** Although you can fake poise, comfort, and security, you can't fake skills and knowledge. It's a critical difference. Faking confidence during a nerve-racking sales meeting, for example, keeps the focus on your abilities, and in the end, you'll gain an authentic sense of grace under pressure. Pretending that you can hand-knit 500 sweaters for Bloomingdale's—by next week—will set you up for failure and ultimately undermine your confidence.

- **Earn it through action.** Although visualizations are a great way to start building your mental confidence, there is no substitute for action. Confidence is something you earn and you build through action—and not just any action. The quickest and most effective way to foster your confidence is by following your gut and acting directly on your instincts, value base, and understanding of Who You Think You Are.

- **Follow the leader.** There is nothing wrong and everything right about getting into line and using the confidence, actions, and solutions of others to lead the way. Acquaint yourself with everyone who has succeeded (and not succeeded) at the leap you are about to take. Although no one else can give you confidence, others can sure inspire it!

- **Be prepared.** Really—don't go into a leap without preparation. You might be scared in the face of a challenge, but don't be scared *and* foolish. Failure is difficult, but if you have done everything in your power to prepare, you can walk away with a sense of pride and confidence in knowing you tried your best. I know from my own expe-

strategy*

EVALUATING YOUR LEAP

Inevitably, there are times when you will meet a challenge that will stop you dead in your tracks, and rather than blazing ahead, you seriously have to consider *Am I up for this?* Here are a few questions to help you reach your own conclusion:

- Will the risk or challenge fundamentally improve my life?
- What is the worst-case scenario?
- How will this risk affect those around me?
- Am I excited about this particular opportunity, or am I just ready for a challenge? (Right time, wrong risk)
- Is this the right risk for me to take at this time in my life? (Wrong time, right risk)
- Is my intuition or "gut" telling me anything I need to take note of about this opportunity?

rience that if you fail due to your own lack of foresight, effort, and preparation, you can seriously erode your confidence level.

- **Go big.** Confidence-building is sort of like investing your money: The bigger the risk, the greater the potential for return. Consider taking your risk or challenge one step further. Your confidence will grow in direct proportion to the size of the challenge.

> If you act like you know what you're doing, you can do anything you want—except neurosurgery.
>
> —Sharon Stone

Leaps Always Worth Taking

The most important risks in life have nothing to do with climbing mountains, getting up on stage, or starting your own business. These risks, although perhaps

You win or lose the match before you even go out there.

—Venus Williams

not obvious or heart-stopping, are in fact the foundation of your Quest for Success and the most important leaps you can take. Defining success for yourself, admitting you don't know, and standing up for yourself—these are just a few of the risks (and yes they are risks) that, left untaken, undermine your sense of confidence, integrity, and self. These are the leaps that make all other risks possible.

Follow your heart.

Ask for what you deserve.

Accept responsibility.

Stand up for yourself.

Stand up for someone else.

Admit you don't know.

Think the unthinkable.

After the Leap

I wouldn't necessarily jump off a bridge again, but I've never, ever, regretted it. Kel showed me that you can actually become set in your leaping ways. I'm not usually a bungee-jumping, skydiving, swim-with-sharks type of girl. I was comfortable taking leaps in my professional life, but I had yet to push myself physically, and I could definitely use a little shove in my personal life.

In the end, that heart-bursting free fall helped me define what risk really is. Sometimes you will do things that scare you, but you don't really recognize or celebrate them as leaps. The bungee jump was a clear-cut, textbook risk. It helped me define and acknowledge the other leaps I had taken in my past and the risks I would take in the future.

When you truly appreciate and respect your risks, you fuel your own bravery. Confidence follows the adrenaline surge. Every time you step off the mental (or physical) platform, your sense of courage gets stronger. You get a little more comfortable with fear, and soon, a voice starts whispering *This is fun*.

PART TWO

FACING YOUR FEARS

You know the dream—the one where you are being chased and you simply can't run fast enough. Have you ever actually turned around to look at what's on your heels?

Risk wouldn't be risk without the fear. Most of us can feel fear lurking in our lives, but we can't put our finger on it. It hovers around and behind us, almost like a ghost, something we're afraid to stop and examine for fear that it will consume us. I'm a firm believer that you can't tackle what you don't know. The critical part of living with and thriving through the unique stimulation, excitement, and adrenaline that comes with fear is actually defining and facing what you're afraid of.

> Courage is very important. Like a muscle, it is strengthened by use.
> —Ruth Gordon

Your fears are uniquely yours and yours alone (I'm not sure if that's good news or bad). I've taken some of the fears I hear discussed by young women most frequently and have explored them in this next section. You might see yourself in the fear of actually learning your limits, discomfort, success, failure, or rejection—or your fear might be revealed through the "What if?" exercise.

What If?

You will be laughed off the stage, your boss will run up one side of you and down the other, you'll have to give up your weekends—what are you afraid of? We all live with a nagging sense of what might actually become real in our lives.

Career Confession

WHAT IF?

What an opportunity—a high-profile international position at my company. But the first time I thought about traveling for a year, I cried. I was just terrified by the thought of leaving home for that long, to go that far away (Asia, India, Africa). My fear might sound silly to the many women who are naturally adventurous spirits, but for me, thirty years old, with a good job, a husband, close family ties, saving for our first home, and maybe children soon after—the thought upset me, scared me, and generally threw me for a loop.

Thanks to time, openness, supportive friends, and lots of discussions with my husband, I opened my mind to the possibilities. I played the "What if . . . ?" game with myself. I asked myself *What if this didn't scare me? What if I decided to embrace this idea for a moment? What would I allow myself to think then? Where could I let my mind go? What did I want to see of the world?* And finally, *What would really change or be jeopardized if I did this? What great things could come of this experience?*

I started to profile the fear behind my initial reactions, and I realized it was simply fear of the unknown in the world and the unknowns within me. After all, this was not "the plan." I simply had to take a leap of faith and trust myself, my husband, and the world!

Mary, corporate recruiter

> Even from a very early age, I knew I didn't want to miss out on anything life had to offer just because it might be considered dangerous.
> —Nicole Kidman

When risk is involved, fears reflect our expectations—both good and bad. Just as we fear utter failure, success could bring its own set of challenges, and our mind reels with the possibilities. Although the majority of your fears will never become reality, asking yourself "What if?" can prepare you to handle uncertainty. It also helps you take more deliberate risks. If you're willing to accept even the worst possible outcome, you know it's time to leap.

I know what you're thinking. *I'm already afraid. Why do I want to spend time thinking about my fears?* But fears are often—no, almost always—

> It is far more difficult to kill a phantom than a reality.
> —Virginia Woolf

worse than the ultimate outcome. When you honestly confront what you fear and why, it can actually feel invigorating. The sense of hovering distraction disappears, leaving you free to focus on the next step and live fully through your Quest.

Fear of Discomfort

There is a quote from author Barbara Sher that makes me feel both reassured and uneasy at the same time. She writes, "What will determine the course of your life more than any other one thing is whether or not you are willing to tolerate necessary discomfort."

As a Wildly Sophisticated woman dedicated to excellence and stretching to test your potential, you will experience times of discomfort. Fear is unnerving. Success takes work. Of course it's easier to watch *Law & Order* than study that extra hour for your exam or hit the gym.

But anticipating the effort is always worse than the reality. Discipline gets easier with practice, and inevitably, the discomfort involved is far less than you anticipated. You can spend your days—and even your life—dreading the down-and-dirty work of creating success, but once you get started, you'll be happy you made the effort. Every time you take the steps you need to take, and live through the temporary "discomfort," you're building confidence and discipline. Stand taller knowing you've truly committed yourself to reaching your goals.

strategy∗

Think about all the obstacles and triumphs that could emerge as you pursue your goals. What if your business loan is denied? What if you don't get the promotion you're hoping for? What if you do? What if you achieve more success than you ever dreamed possible? Most of us have deep-seated fears, imagined obstacles, and personal challenges that we'd rather not identify. You will gain tremendous power by getting them all out.

- Identify key goals, dreams, or intentions.
- Underneath each, write out all your "What if?" questions in reference both to success and failure.
- After each "What if?" answer your questions starting with the words "I will." What if my business loan is denied? I will ask questions and understand the problem. I will re-work my application. I will apply at another bank. I will talk with my parents about a short-term loan.

Note: The process of identifying your "What if?" questions can be overwhelming. I would not suggest you attempt this exercise the same week you get laid off, your boyfriend dumps you, and you've got a bad case of PMS. You might also want to do this activity with a friend and set a maximum time limit.

Fear of Success

I used to read about fear of success limiting our ability to achieve our dreams and quite honestly thought *Bullshit*. What about success isn't desirable? Why wouldn't we want to be successful?

I only started to think about fear of success one day as my best friend Jenn

Career Confession

WHAT HAVE I DONE?

I've worked at the same firm for three years now. Last month, my supervisor moved to Alaska (don't ask . . .), and I knew I could land his position. I flew into action. I drew up some new promotional strategies and updated our client list. I schemed. I worked my ass off. I fantasized about leaving the cubicle ghetto for an office with a real door and a window.

Well, I got the job all right, but now I've also got insomnia, panic attacks, and a whole new understanding of the word *stress*. My best friend says I'll soon feel more comfortable—I just have to give it time. I'm counting on her to be right. Either that or I'll have to start putting Pepto Bismol in my coffee.

Ashley, public relations specialist

and I were discussing our next career moves. So much of our long-time friendship had been based in supporting each other on our journey. While we would cheer each other on through the hard times, something interesting had started to happen between us with the introduction of the good times. Our careers, in different industries, started to have moments of great success, and the dynamic of our relationship started to change. We supported each other unconditionally, but we were both a little afraid to be left behind. There came a time when I worried that success would change our relationship. I started to wonder, quite frankly, if the price was too high.

When we fear success, it's often due to underlying anxieties about change. As much as we long to reach a target or achieve a goal, our current situation is comfortable. We worry our entire

> There came a time when the risk to remain tight in the bud was more painful than the risk it took to blossom.
>
> —Anaïs Nin

> I'm afraid of what I am, what I'm not, what I might become, what I might never become.
>
> —Michelle Pfeiffer

life could change and we might somehow lose control. For example, you may dream of starting a family, but you dread abandoning your career, stretching your marriage too thin, or losing track of yourself. Or maybe landing that incredible film

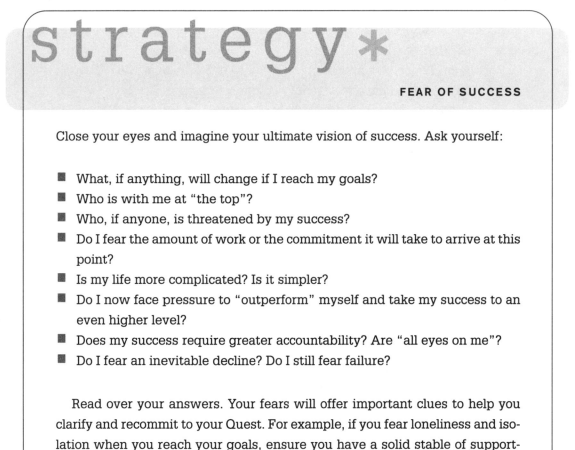

strategy*

FEAR OF SUCCESS

Close your eyes and imagine your ultimate vision of success. Ask yourself:

- What, if anything, will change if I reach my goals?
- Who is with me at "the top"?
- Who, if anyone, is threatened by my success?
- Do I fear the amount of work or the commitment it will take to arrive at this point?
- Is my life more complicated? Is it simpler?
- Do I now face pressure to "outperform" myself and take my success to an even higher level?
- Does my success require greater accountability? Are "all eyes on me"?
- Do I fear an inevitable decline? Do I still fear failure?

Read over your answers. Your fears will offer important clues to help you clarify and recommit to your Quest. For example, if you fear loneliness and isolation when you reach your goals, ensure you have a solid stable of supporters—people who are with you for the long haul. If you worry about building a complicated, chaotic life, remind yourself that you will create success and live on your own terms, your way.

role could mean you have to move away, leave your family, and start a new, potentially lonely life.

We might also fear the sheer effort it will take to achieve success, and realize that if we do reach the top, we will have to work even harder and achieve even more. For a lot of us, success generates even more fear and anxiety than failure. But acknowledging our fears around success is a powerful way to remove the roadblocks. Life offers enough challenges. Get out of your own way.

Fear of Failure

When I think about "successful" failures, Diane von Furstenberg instantly comes to mind. Talk about failing with style—and emerging stronger on the other side.

At age twenty-nine, Diane von Furstenberg hit a fashion gold mine when she created the wrap dress—a sexy yet practical wardrobe staple that quickly gained iconic status. Von Furstenberg's business grew with lightning speed, churning out more than 25,000 dresses a week at the height of their popularity. But she had licensed her merchandise to everyone and anyone who was interested, and the dresses eventually lost their value. She descended from the cover of *Newsweek* magazine to practically begging suppliers to carry her designs. With all her strength—and all her money—von Furstenberg ignored the critics and spent ten years rebuilding her fashion reputation. In 1997, she re-launched the wrap dress to a new generation of women. Once again, women everywhere snapped up the dresses and turned her brand into a sought-after label.

When you think about it, in the face of failure we most often have two fears: disappointing others and disappointing ourselves. While both fears can be very real and very powerful, keep one

> There is no downside to success.
> —Sherry Lansing

thing in mind: Disappointment and failure are not the same thing. Disappointment is a *feeling*—an emotion—to manage and eventually get over. Failure itself is an *experience* to learn from.

Career Confession

SWEATY PALMS

As a teenager, I studied the violin and competed in music festivals around the city. I learned to feel comfortable performing for other people and especially for judges who gleefully scrutinized every single note. I also learned to be comfortable with fear.

As each competition began, I usually left the room to pace around, review my music, and warm up my hands—which inevitably lost all blood flow right before my turn to play. I was always nervous, but I began to track and understand my pre-performance jitters.

I realized cold hands were normal—for me. A pair of icy mitts was something I could count on, because my nervousness was partly fear, but also excitement and anticipation. I began to understand that my nerves were not only normal, they were actually helpful. The subtle stress of performing pushed me into a higher state of awareness, and I *always* played better in competition than my best efforts in the practice room.

Except if my hands were sweaty. Clammy palms reflected more than nervous excitement—they meant I was downright scared, and it was my own damn fault. Sweaty palms meant I was unprepared.

That destructive fear undercut my confidence.

Kristin, event coordinator

> You may be disappointed if you fail, but you are doomed if you don't try.
>
> —Beverly Sills

Disappointing Others

This is the public side of failure, and it's mainly tied to our ego: *What will people think of me? Will they still like me? Will they think I'm a loser? I don't want to let anyone down.*

strategy*

Close your eyes and imagine the risk you want to take. Without getting anxious or upset, think about what it would mean to "fail." Be gentle with yourself, but be honest.

- If you did, indeed, fail, what would you do next?
- What other options would emerge?
- How would you handle the failure?

Think about another time when you have failed.

- Why did you fail?
- How did you handle the experience?
- What did you learn?
- How did the failure affect where you are now?

Sometimes I think our culture considers the word *failure* more offensive than any possible string of four-letter words. If failure was a movie, it would definitely be rated NC-17. We are obsessed with celebrating victories rather than honoring and respecting failures. When you work past a knee-jerk reaction to the idea of failure, it can help you understand that failure is definitely not the end of the world. No matter what happens, you can handle it. Even better—failure will make you stronger.

One-on-One

Letting Go of Fear

Before setting out to build my business, I spent a week secluded on beautiful Vancouver Island. The intention for the reprieve was to decide if I was actually up to the challenge—if I was prepared to live with the imbalance it would require. Over the course of the week, I began to realize my decision was impeded by the fear of not actually being able to complete the task. In a moment of New Age mania—the sound of ocean will do that to you—I wrote down all my fears about committing to the process, burned them in the fireplace, then walked the ashes to the water's edge and released them into the breeze. What can you do to ceremoniously let go of your fear?

> Life is truly known only to those who suffer, lose, endure adversity, and stumble from defeat to defeat.
> —Anaïs Nin

Diane von Furstenberg's crash was extremely public. The whole world was watching! But it's critical to maintain perspective. People forgive and, more important, they forget. The next time you're afraid to take on a challenge for fear of embarrassing, discrediting, or humiliating yourself, remember these four simple, timeless realities:

- Everyone is infinitely more concerned with themselves than they are with you.

- Everyone is attracted to people who expose vulnerability—it makes you real.

- No one is judging you as harshly as you're judging yourself.

- Everyone loves a comeback story.

Disappointing Ourselves

When it comes down to it, it's our fear of disappointing ourselves that stops us dead in our tracks. I don't know too many people who go out there actually looking to fail, but when it happens (which it inevitably will) the learning, growth, and power on the other side makes the whole process well worthwhile.

- Failure that makes you feel ashamed or embarrassed offers the most valuable learning experiences. The more it hurts, the more you remember it.

- If you're fully prepared and you've tried your best, failure won't wound your self-esteem.

- You can always come back stronger, smarter, and more powerful.

Fear of the Spotlight

Sometimes our greatest fears go past sheer success or failure. When we put ourselves "out there" and accept a challenge, we become vulnerable. Suddenly, all eyes will be focused directly on us, and we will have to answer to a firing squad of critics and casual observers. Leading the way, standing out from the crowd, positioning yourself at the top—whatever you want to call it, breaking away from the pack requires a special kind of risk.

> If you love large, you've got to hurt large. If you've got a lot of light, you've probably got an equal amount of darkness.
> —Sarah McLachlan

Stretch Assignments

The most challenging project pushes your limits and tests your skills. Seeking and committing to a "stretch assignment" is a risk—one that is not only well worth taking in terms of the personal opportunity to grow, but absolutely

strategy*

STRETCH YOURSELF

Spend some time identifying the next step on your Quest for Success.

- Who is currently the leader in the position you are aspiring to reach? Whether she is in your organization or not, ask her for an information interview. Ask her about the skill sets and talents she is utilizing in her position. If you aren't able to find someone to talk with, log onto Monster.com and look for a related job title and read through the description.
- Make a list of the skill sets, experiences, and abilities you need to build in order to launch yourself to the next level.
- Finally, look at your current position and organization and identify which projects will offer you the opportunity to build the skills you have identified.

necessary if you are committed to breaking out. Following are several guidelines to support you in identifying and succeeding at the stretch assignment.

Stretch assignments are everywhere. Beyond letting your superiors know you are on the lookout for the opportunity to contribute beyond your current job description, keep your eyes open. What you are looking for: Start with your boss. What is she struggling with? Can you build your skills and help her out at the same time? Is there a level of dysfunction or inefficiency within your organization that you can (tactfully) identify and suggest you'd like to work on rectifying?

While stretching allows you to try on different skills, opportunities, and experiences, you want to be sure you're focusing your stretch. In most instances, you are stretching in conjunction with your current job responsibilities. Succeeding at a stretch assignment takes time and energy—your most valuable commodities. Take the time to pre-plan your stretch.

Be a Leader

Don't be afraid to involve others in your stretch. One of the greatest misconceptions about the stretch assignment is that you have to do it alone to get the recognition you desire. Operate abundantly, and rather than horde your opportunity, let others know what you are working on and invite them to join you. Sharing your stretch is going to help you in three specific ways:

> **Power is nothing unless you can turn it into influence.**
> —Condoleezza Rice

- You can get more accomplished with the help of others. Everyone has different skills and talents that can enhance your project and widen your own professional repertoire. You'll gain new ideas and approaches you might not have even considered on your own.

- Not everyone is a natural leader and will necessarily be looking for the opportunity to excel as you are. Sharing your initiative will not only show your superiors you have the capacity to lead (which is an amazing professional attribute), but you also will incur the respect and loyalty of your co-workers who won't forget your willingness to bring them in on the deal—think karma.

- The goal of the stretch assignment is to build your skill base. You can do this more efficiently through the learning and experiences of others.

Other People's Fear

Every Sunday morning I call home. My family lives across the country, and thanks to the combination of distance and my nontraditional choices, their fears, worries, and anxieties on my behalf travel loud and clear across the phone lines. This morning, I'm already feeling a bit scared and overwhelmed. The last thing I needed was to have my fears compounded. As I hung up the phone, I

> No pessimist ever discovered the secrets of the stars, or sailed to an uncharted land, or opened a new heaven to the human spirit.
>
> —Helen Keller

remembered a lesson I apparently still need to learn.

The lesson? There are people who love and want to protect you with all their heart. When they express fear for you, it comes from the most compassionate of places. Regardless, you need to be able to distance yourself from their fears. Let your family and friends know that while you appreciate their concern, it's more than a little disconcerting when they remind you that going back to school could leave you homeless and in heavy-duty debt. In the face of challenge and risk, your own fears are more than enough to contend with, thank you very much.

❊   ❊   ❊

The night before my presentation in Atlanta, I lay in bed completely paralyzed with terror. I certainly wasn't sleeping, so I got up and started to write through the fear. I wrote about why I was scared, what I imagined happening, and what I had to present. Slowly, a bigger truth emerged: My real challenge, and my purpose, was to simply work through this experience. I realized that the presentation topic itself was irrelevant. I could stand up there and explain how to choose the perfect black turtleneck, but I had to go through with the whole process of pushing my limits—the excitement, the fear, and the relief—to grab the wisdom waiting on the other side.

I had already started gravitating toward career development, this book, and my business, and somewhere in my gut, I knew I had to embrace the experience in order to understand it and to write about it. I could live through my fear because it was attached to a greater dream—something I wanted to do with all my heart.

The presentation went fine. Actually, it was anticlimactic. The visions and fears swimming through my head beforehand were a billion times worse than any slight public speaking jitters. And I learned another important lesson: Everyone's scared. Fear never goes away. We're all human, and everyone has to psych themselves up to meet the crowds or critics. Face your fears. Trust yourself and take the leap!

5

Are You Prepared?

Investing in Yourself

I've locked myself in the airport bathroom, and I'm not coming out. I'm scared. Not nervous. Not a little uneasy. Not worried. Scared.

Hours earlier I sat on a plane marveling at the adventure before me. As the airline attendant handed me my Diet Coke, he asked, "So what are your plans while you're in Singapore?"

Delighted for a break in my personal reverie, I replied, "Actually, I'm just stopping over on my way to Nepal."

"Nepal?" he echoed excitedly. "You must be meeting some friends."

"No. Actually, I just graduated and all my friends are already working."

"Where are you staying?"

"I'm not sure, but I've got my copy of the Lonely Planet.*"*

His eyes betrayed a sense of empathetic fear as he asked tentatively, "Have you arranged for someone to pick you up?"

"No. I'm thinking I'll figure it out when I get there."

"Are you at all prepared?"

I suddenly wished he would stop with the questions.

This may be a peculiar story through which to introduce the concept of preparation as it relates to career development, but the experience taught me three critical things about preparation.

- **Sometimes, you need an objective perspective.** Although preparation is 100 percent your responsibility (I couldn't have very well asked the airline attendant to help me plan my trip at that point), sometimes you need someone else, someone from the outside, someone with experience, to help you objectively assess your level of preparedness.

- **Preparation becomes *more* important as your success grows, not less.** The more successful you become in your career, the more diligent you need to be in investing in yourself through preparation. Unique, challenge-filled, life-enhancing experiences require preparation. I made it through the trip to Nepal, and it was good, but it wasn't amazing. I didn't pre-book tours, arrange a Buddhist mediation, or schedule a full-body massage. I missed out on some incredible opportunities.

- **Not being prepared is at the root of fear.** The better prepared you are, the better able you are to tackle all the risk and challenge I discussed in Chapter Four. My lack of preparation scared me, and my feelings of fear and trepidation prevented me from truly living the experience (although I did make it out of the bathroom). This same concept applies to your career development. There will be moments (forget moments, even months) when you will be scared, and it will be your sense of preparedness that will give you the confidence and commitment you need to not only persevere but succeed on your Quest.

> **It's important to give it all you have while you have the chance.**
> —Shania Twain

Oprah has a great line, "Luck is a matter of preparation meeting opportunity." Great and meaningful work does not just happen. Positive thinking helps, as does the right degree and solid work experience, but without the essential preparation, you will not reach your intended goal. The opportunity part is easy. The world of work is filled with possibilities—you simply need the preparation to reach out and grab them!

Your career development is your responsibility. No one is going to do this for you. Preparation is a form of investment and proves to both yourself and others that you believe you're worth it. How can you ask others (employers, mentors, bosses) to invest in you when you are not committed to investing in yourself? Preparation provides you with an empowering foundation for self-reliance and personal responsibility.

The days of the cradle-to-grave employer and resting on past success and achievements are long gone. The world of work is changing faster than ever. You are likely to experience about six to ten career shifts in your lifetime. Companies go bankrupt, and layoffs are a reality. That's why preparation is the key to not only surviving, but excelling through this state of flux. Be on top of your game, and differentiate yourself with a level of preparation that ensures you are ready for your "lucky" break. Wildly Sophisticated women will commit themselves to "Be Prepared"—for the opportunities, for the failures, for the effort, and for the success.

This chapter explores the concept of career management and how to ensure you (not a boss or your friends or your parents) are consciously directing your working life. Next, we look at situations such as résumé preparation and salary negotiations. Your career is a Quest—a journey—and this chapter will give you the map you need to maximize and enjoy every single moment.

Career Confession

OFF THE PATH

With a night finally free from the pressures of work, I was delighted to discover the latest issue of *Elle* had reached the newsstands. I picked up a wonderful Australian Shiraz to savor as I lay in the bath checking out the latest fashions, learning secret beauty tips, and reading that exclusive interview with Jennifer Lopez.

As I began to read about J Lo, I couldn't stop thinking about my own career. I mean here's Jennifer Lopez—young, beautiful, and from perfume to movie stardom—the consummate career woman. I couldn't help thinking, *How did she do it? And better yet, how can I do it, too?* As I'm preparing to celebrate my twenty-eighth birthday, I'm struck with the reality that I've spent the last couple years floundering on a directionless path. As I look around at the lives and careers of women my age, I'm starting to wonder if I shouldn't be taking more initiative.

Lena, sales manager

PART ONE
CAREER MANAGEMENT

Many of us don't start to consciously think about our career development until we hit a milestone birthday, get laid off, or come to the realization that we're not going to make the Olympic team. The reality is, you need to start strategically managing your career—today. Don't let the natural ebb and flow of life exert the upper hand in your career development. If you're working from the Wildly Sophisticated perspective of Starting Personal to Be Professional, you understand that your professional development is not just about your career, it's about you—and you are an investment worth making.

As a career manager, there are three primary misconceptions I hear all the time:

- **I'm not in crisis, my job is fine—I don't need any help.** The last thing you want to be doing in a time of a job crisis is to finally start thinking about career management. In fact, if you are invested in your career development, you are infinitely less likely to actually hit a crisis point.

- **Career managers are for people who are unsuccessful or people who are stuck.** Tiger Woods, Katie Couric, Venus Williams—do these people look stuck to you? Need I say more?

- **My human resources person will manage my career development.** No, no, and no. You and your career are precious commodities. Are you seriously going to trust the woman on the third floor who wouldn't know you from a hole in the wall to take responsibility for your success? This is your responsibility and your responsibility alone.

Okay, so now you're convinced—and I've got some good news. Career management is not as daunting as it might sound. It's simply a commitment to take your career seriously, to invest in yourself, and to take responsibility for your professional growth. As I have already discussed, the world of work is changing at an ever-faster pace, and the days of a gold watch at retirement are firmly anchored in the past. Taking an active role in your career development is no longer an option; it's a necessity. You need to think strategically about where you've been, where you are, and where you're going.

The following questions will help you get started. Think of these questions as the building blocks of your career. Regardless of industry, age, or experience level, these questions will help you assess your current position and make strategic plans for the future.

Why a Career Manager?

I'm a big believer that we need to take an active, invested role in our development at all times, but an even bigger believer that there are points along the

strategy*

You have an extraordinary opportunity to use the initial years of your career to build a strong foundation for success. On a scale of 1 to 10, where 10 is total satisfaction and 1 is complete dissatisfaction, rate the following dimensions of your career. Keep in mind that you might need to create both general and element-specific rankings. For example, although you might have a terrific relationship with your boss, you might feel unconnected with your co-workers. Yet overall, you might be satisfied with your work relationship "package."

Relationships with your boss / co-workers / peers

Do your relationships enrich your work experience? Enliven the workplace? Inspire and encourage your work?

1   2   3   4   5   6   7   8   9   10

Learning / challenges

Does your work stretch and test your limits? Does it help you grow and provide opportunities to learn?

1   2   3   4   5   6   7   8   9   10

Self-Expression / contribution

Does your work allow you to express who you think you are? Does it help you explore your values and dreams? Does it allow you to express your unique strengths, talents, and abilities?

1   2   3   4   5   6   7   8   9   10

Compensation

Are you satisfied with your salary or pay scale? How about other benefits such as professional development courses, lectures, or conference opportunities? Do you have enough vacation time? Do you have enough time and scheduling flexibility?

1   2   3   4   5   6   7   8   9   10

Day-to-day realities

Are you happy with the time commitment involved in your work? Do you work a desirable number of hours per week? Is your work environment (physical space) pleasant? How long is your commute to and from work?

1   2   3   4   5   6   7   8   9   10

Outlook

Does your work offer the opportunity to advance? Can you move up the ranks, so to speak, or laterally, into different roles and responsibilities? Is your work taking you where you want to go? Helping you achieve your goals?

1   2   3   4   5   6   7   8   9   10

Look at your rankings. Unless you're J. Lo, I'm going to suspect you have some mixed numbers. Actually, even she would have areas for improvement—less paparazzi, more vacation time, more challenging film roles. You get the picture.

This strategy is not designed to make you feel depressed or suggest you should immediately quit your job. Instead, examining your work as a whole composed of many different parts should highlight the benefits of career management. Even if you adore your work, there are always areas to stretch and improve. Capitalize on what's satisfying, and put that knowledge to use on those areas at the low end of the scale.

Quest when you need a career manager—someone who you pay to push your limits, guide your progress, and provide information and resources that help take you to the next level.

A career manager is someone who objectively helps you build success. Someone who has the resources, experiences, and fundamental understanding of what it takes to both create and nurture a successful career. While a career manager starts with an in-depth analysis of Who You Think You Are, she will also provide you with concrete direction and resources. I created Wildly Sophisticated Media as a career building business because I needed this kind of help in my own professional life. I wanted someone who had the resources, information, and networks to propel me further on my own Quest for Success. I want to give young women the tools I wasn't able to access when I needed them most.

Build Me Up

Every second morning, I grab my DKNY duffle bag and hit the gym—not just any gym, but a personal training facility. As I open the door to the some days torture chamber, some days oasis, Barb is waiting for me like a dutiful dog (I'm sure she'll appreciate that description). Barb always looks refreshed, she's always enthusiastic, and she's always ready to get started, which is both disconcerting and invigorating at 6 A.M. It's not that I can't work out on my own, it's that I don't want to, at least right now. I also know that I'll get toned biceps a lot faster with Barb's expertise than if I fumble around with the dumbbells by myself.

I've used my experience with Barb as an analogy for career management, because I think it's the best way to explain—without boring you to tears—how professional support can boost your career. If you are considering investing in a career manager, here are a few of the perks:

- **It's all about you.** This is the thing—I don't have to ask about Barb's workout yesterday; I don't have to feel guilty about taking too much of her time; I don't have to think about what move comes next. Having a manager, someone who is 100 percent focused on your success, is critical at points along your Quest. There is something both wonderfully decadent and empowering about experiencing someone focused wholly and completely on your success. This is a two-way relationship, but after you've signed the check, it's all about you.

- **You're invested.** *Before a personal trainer:* Alarm blares in my ear, I roll over and hit the sleep button, then wake up an hour later. *After a personal trainer:* Alarm blares, I roll over, consider hitting the sleep button, remember I'm going to be charged for my workout whether I'm there or not, and get out of bed.

  Incentive and motivation come in all different shapes and sizes, and sixty bucks is sixty bucks. When I first started my career management practice, I would meet women who needed my help but couldn't afford it. Because I was as excited about their potential success as they were, I'd allow them to participate in a workshop for free. Only one woman had to show up the next Saturday with a new pair of Manolo Blahnik boots and a hangover for me to realize the problem: We value what we pay for. Your career development is an investment and investment requires sacrifice. Today, I will still meet women who can't afford to participate in a workshop, but even if they can't afford to pay in cash, we trade services. If you want to create success, invest in your career. Invest your time in learning a new skill, spend an evening in the library or online, or sign up for a course.

- **You get an objective perspective on your limits.** There are some mornings when I absolutely, positively believe with everything in me that I cannot possibly do one more rep. But Barb, with exactly the same level of conviction, thinks I can. The bottom line is that you know yourself best, but in my experience, sometimes we don't want to admit to ourselves that, *Yeah, I probably could do a bit more.* A career manager can help you see yourself more clearly.

- **You have a cheerleader.** "One more. You can do it!" In my mind I'm thinking, *How about you get down here on all fours and kick your fu*%$#g leg for the one hundredth time?* But in reality, I really appreciate the support. A manager's role is to push you on, to motivate and inspire you to action.

- **You have a professional.** I don't know how muscle groups work together to build strength. I don't know the best sequences for interval training. I don't know how many reps it takes to exhaust a muscle. You know what? I don't care. What I do care about is building a healthy body, and I would much rather focus my efforts on performing the moves Barb has strategically designed to help me reach my goal. Your Quest is going to be filled with thousands of options, choices, challenges, and opportunities. Hiring a career manager who can objectively help you define your goal, accurately assess the best way of getting you there, and provide you with a level of expertise that allows you to focus your energy, attention, and resources is an excellent way to create success.

How to Find a Career Manager

This is a new and growing field, so the labels can get confusing. You might find career managers under the terms *career builder, career adviser,* or *career coach.*

You can find career managers:

- **On the web.** Our Wildly Sophisticated website (www.wildlysophisticated. com) offers links to great career managers around the country.

- **By word of mouth.** If you know of anyone who has used a career manager, ask for their name and contact information. Even if you don't click with that specific person, you can ask for referrals to other career professionals in your area.

- **Through resource centers.** Call your local board of trade, business networking group, or college and academic resource centers. Alumni associations and professional development boards may also have links to career managers.

- **Through the ICF.** The International Coach Federation (www.coach federation.org) is a professional association for more than 5,000 member coaches in 36 countries. They also have a searchable directory that can help you find a reputable career coach or manager in your area.

As with any professional service, career coaches (and career managers) should come with a buyer beware tag. Think about getting your hair cut. You could visit a top-notch salon where your stylist has twenty years of experience and a wall of international awards. Or you could surrender your tresses to Mistee, who just finished a Sophomore Beauty Culture course and is now cutting hair in her parents' basement. It's up to you. There are amazing, incredibly well-qualified coaches out there and others who simply make a website, get some business cards, and wait for the money to roll in.

PART TWO
CREATING GOALS

With or without a career manager, setting goals is one of the first steps toward investing in your career. Goals not only provide a sense of direction and purpose but, perhaps more important, they give us a sense of hope—a reason to keep moving and a vision to move toward.

> I have the same goal I've had since I was a girl. I want to rule the world.
> —Madonna

Although we usually consider the accomplishment of our goals as indicating the end of our journey, the actual process of establishing and regularly evaluating your career progress is an amazing part of the Quest. Of all the young women I've worked with, the creation of goals and a clear plan for execution is a primary differentiator between success and failure. Without goals, how can you prepare? It's essential to know your target before you start throwing the darts.

All Goals are Not Created Equal

This might sound bizarre, but all goals are not created equal. Here are a few specific guidelines to help create your own goals.

Your Goals Should Come from You

On one miserable morning, exhausted, tired, and simply sick of working toward my goal, I asked myself a simple question: *Do you want to quit?* I had it all worked out in my mind, the rationale I would use with friends and family who knew of my goal, and how I would extract myself from my obligations. I had envisioned exactly how I could quit. The thing was, I didn't want to. When faced with the question, there was something so deep within me, so startling attached to my sense of Who I Think I Am that I simply could not give up.

> My parents wanted me to be a lawyer. But I don't think I would have been very happy. I'd be in front of the jury singing.
>
> —Jennifer Lopez

That experience taught me that the more closely your goal is allied with Who You Think You Are, the stronger its foundation and the more likely you are to succeed. Create goals that correspond with your values, sense of integrity, and meaning in life. Ask yourself:

- What do I want to contribute to the world?

- What do I stand for?

- What do I want to be known for?

- What natural talents do I possess that I want to share with the world through my work?

Your Goals Should Reflect an Intense Desire

"Hey Mom," I would yell into the house from the front door. "Can I go play with Lisa?"

"Whatever your heart's desire," my mom would call back. As many times as I heard the expression as a kid, I would always stop dead in my tracks with sheer delight. Whatever my heart's desire—could it be possible? I'm here to tell you it is possible. In fact, it is essential if you aspire to create career success.

Beyond creating a goal that is true to you, the next step is to attach your goal to an intense desire. Desire is the fuel behind your goals. Desire is the feeling that keeps you up at night and compels you to wake up early and work through lunch. Desire feeds on intensity, and intensity feeds on detail. Your desire is attached to a vision of the result of your efforts. Ask yourself:

> Nothing contributes so much to tranquilize the mind as a steady purpose—a point on which the soul may fix its intellectual eye.
> —Mary Shelley

- Think about the most exciting, joyful, and fulfilling day I have ever lived. What elements of that day do I want to regularly experience through my work?

- How many hours a week do I want to work?

- How much money do I want to be paid?

- How many weeks of vacation do I want to take each year?

- What kind of environment do I want to work in?

> The price of self-destiny is never cheap and in certain circumstances it is unthinkable. But to achieve the marvelous, it is precisely the unthinkable that must be thought.
>
> —Tom Robbins

Your Goals Should Help You Achieve Your Unthinkables

The quote on this page by Tom Robbins changed my life. Your experience in life is directly tied to your capacity to dream big and believe in your ability to achieve the marvelous. You might suspect an unthinkable goal is too big to dream of and wish for, but I bet you've already experienced and succeeded at unthinkables and don't even know it. Unthinkables expand the mind and encourage us to dream beyond our estimated capability.

- Think about a time when you have surprised yourself, a time when your efforts created something that at one point would have been unthinkable. Describe the situation and your feelings in as much detail as possible.

- Think outside the box. Stretch your imagination to its furthest reaches and ask yourself this: *What, at this stage in my life, feels absolutely unattainable—what is my unthinkable?*

From Whirling to Planning

As you begin to more clearly define your goals, you might go through a period of what I call whirling. Whirling occurs when your mind quite literally whirls with ideas, opportunities, potential scenarios, fears—you name it. At first, this period of whirling is quite exciting. You let your mind open to possibilities, and your ideas begin to layer and take amazing form. There is a point—though often you're way past it before you realize you've hit it—when you begin to feel overwhelmed and anxious. I've seen people with particularly large dreams whirl for well over a year, unsure of where to get started—how to get out of their head and into action.

One-on-One

A Rolling Stone

Gathers no moss . . . or fear or doubts or emotional roadblocks. Keep your momentum. Stay in motion and keep working toward your goals. Even if you work full-time or keep a crazy schedule, realize that just ten minutes a day can help propel you forward. You don't need a two-week spa vacation to finally start those product sketches. Draw one thing tonight. Do it for fifteen minutes, and do it again tomorrow. You'll be amazed how far momentum will carry you and how it begins to open up the road ahead. Taking daily action will also prevent a backlog of inhibition, fear, and negative energy. It doesn't matter how much time you actually commit. What counts is that you're doing something *now*, and you can use that knowledge to boost your confidence. Keep rolling.

Whirling feels like a hurricane of ideas in your head. After deciding you want to be a journalist, for example, your mind whips itself into a brainstorming frenzy: *I could go to London and work for the* Times. *I could be a CNN correspondent. Maybe I should go back to school or start writing freelance pieces for my local paper. I could get an internship or start as a researcher.* Moving from the whirling hurricane into concrete plans is the last stage before setting goals, which nails down detailed steps and time lines to help you achieve specific milestones.

If you've been whirling for an extended period of time, you might need to work through this process with a career manager or someone you trust to help guide your steps and give you some perspective. If this idea relates to a new business, starting a family, or a change in career direction, ask someone who has the experience or frame of reference to help you out.

- **Let it all out.** Take your ideas and transcribe your thoughts—all of them—onto paper. In my experience, this piece of paper quite literally can look like a whirl, with ideas and thoughts thrown all over the page. Don't worry about being neat or orderly in your writing. Just get everything that is whirling around in your mind down on paper.

- **Find the heart.** Somewhere on this paper is the heart of your goal or dream. Sometimes it's difficult to identify, but the heart is usually where you started—the original idea. Once you find the core, take another piece of paper and write the primary goal, vision, or dream at the top.

strategy *

EIGHT STEPS TO GOAL SETTING

Here is a simple eight-step formula for achieving goals that you can use for the rest of your career.

1. **Focus on your goal.** Make sure you can see it, feel it, and describe it. Imagine the details. Be as clear as possible.

2. **Put it on paper.** Writing down your goal gives it energy and momentum. Be specific. If you want to start a running program, write down when, where, and how much you will run each day.

3. **Make a time line for your goal, with smaller goals along the way.**

Deadlines will help you take action and create results. For example, if you want to run in a 10K race next June, circle the date on your calendar and write it in your date book. In six months, plan to run in a 5K race.

4. **Write down everything you need to do to achieve your goal.** Some items will be simple (buy new running shoes), while others will be more complicated (research nutrition requirements for runners). Keep your list up to date. Add new tasks or change existing ones as you go.

- **Start organizing.** Take your initial whirl sheet and read it over. Do you see any logical patterns? Create categories: skill development/training, learning/research, conversations/meetings.

- **Review your categories to create a sense of timing.** What goes before and after what? Use your big goal to create the smaller milestone goals.

- **Work it backward.** If your goal is to star in a Hollywood film by age thirty-five, what will you need to do to arrive there? Maybe you need to

5. **Make a plan.** Figure out what tasks to do immediately and what you will do later. Be honest with yourself. Make your plan realistic, but don't sell yourself short. You'll be amazed how much you can do when you combine desire with design.

6. **Start now.** You've created the plan, now do it. Even the smallest steps will feed your momentum and energy. If you hit stumbling blocks, rework your plan and keep going.

7. **Move toward your goal every single day.** Achievement—like finishing a 10K marathon—is the sum total of many smaller steps. Keep on track. If a nasty cold sidelines your running regimen,

use the downtime to plan a new route. Or read a running magazine and pick up some new conditioning tips. Daily actions help you stay committed and will give you strength to nurture your dreams into reality.

8. **Periodically reassess and reevaluate your goal.** What's working? What's not? When you're making progress, it's easy to get caught up in the momentum and forget why you're dragging your butt out of bed each morning in the first place! Knowing you're on the right track will help keep you motivated. Or if your goal has changed along the way, be flexible and adapt to the new vision. Goals are rarely static—they shift to fit Who You Think You Are.

take acting classes, watch great films, act in a local play or independent film, sign an agent, start auditioning, and build your contacts in Hollywood. There are key steps on the way toward your ultimate goal. Plan to take them in succession.

Keeping Plans in Perspective

As important as goals are in the acquisition of your dreams, the reality is, shit happens. If there is one thing I can promise you, it's that the check will take longer to arrive, the offer won't come as soon as you expected, and the project will take infinitely more effort and time than you ever expected. Don't get discouraged. Your goals and plan for execution have to incorporate a level of "give."

> I'm going to college. I don't care if it ruins my career. I'd rather be smart than a movie star.
> —Natalie Portman

Both you and your goals need to be flexible. Life sometimes offers you opportunity that you never could have dreamed of, let alone planned for. Don't let your goals get in the way of life.

PART THREE
DIVE IN

Internships

Before you invest a chunk of change getting a law degree or another piece of paper to frame, you might want to actually spend some time working in the field. Information interviews, online research, industry events—nothing beats actually stepping into the position *now*. Internships and volunteering provide low-commitment, high-intensity opportunities to explore your field of interest. If managed correctly, internships offer an enormous learning curve.

But don't think internships are just for college students or recent grads. One of my workshop participants was a marketing whiz working for a major hotel chain, but she was considering a new industry. She cut her work schedule from five days to four and spent every Friday sampling her prospective new profession. As an experienced professional, you'll command even more respect by taking a potential career shift so seriously. It doesn't matter how old or how established you are. You can always dip your toe and test the waters *before* you dive in.

I won't lie to you. In many cases, internships are not always glamorous—you'll need a pen and paper to get all the skim milk, double shot, extra-hot latte orders—but as with everything, the experience will be what you make it. Your Wildly Sophisticated commitment to excellence and getting over yourself will come in very handy.

How to Find an Internship

Many organizations will post internship opportunities on their websites or through their human resources departments. You can also contact your college or university's career development department or call your alumni association. Just like regular positions, internships often require a full application, interview, and hiring process. The protocol will vary by company and especially by industry.

In my experience, however, the best way to find an internship is to create your own. If there's a particular company you are interested in working for and you feel you have a lot to learn and to contribute—ask! What company wouldn't want an eager, intelligent, and self-motivated young woman to intern with their organization? Many companies are severely understaffed and don't have the time to create structured internship programs. These needy organizations are often thrilled to have some help.

> Action will remove the doubt that theory cannot solve.
> —Tehyi Hsieh

If you land an internship, here are some do's and dont's to keep in mind:

- **Do** treat it like a job you are being paid for. Even if there's no paycheck, your remuneration comes in the form of experience.

- **Don't** take for granted that your supervisor will create an amazing learning experience for you. In all honesty, some companies take interns because they are financially strapped, and more often than not, they have limited time and energy to devote to you.

- **Don't** hole up in your cubicle. Of all the amazing things you can get out of your internship experience, a network of colleagues, mentors, and peers is at the top of the list.

- **Do** take your internship seriously. Your employer is making a significant investment by orchestrating this opportunity. You will tarnish your reputation if you don't take the position seriously and act responsibly.

- **Do** define your employment boundaries. From the internship length to how many hours you will be expected to commit, set some clear boundaries and expectations you cannot only meet, but exceed. *Note:* I've seen employers take advantage of interns, but remember your Wildly Sophisticated perspective of Nothing but the Very Best. It's not okay to pick up your supervisor's kids after school or do her laundry.

- **Don't** be surprised or disappointed if your task list starts out small. Prove through your actions that you are capable of handling more challenging assignments.

- **Do** explore the next steps. What happens if this is a match? What are your mutual goals moving forward? You won't get what you don't ask for. Many people find full-time employment opportunities through their internship positions.

- **Don't** be afraid to ask for feedback. Ask your supervisor to give you some indication of where you're excelling and what you could be doing better or more efficiently.

- **Do** be strategic. What do you want to get out of this experience? What are the specific skill sets you are attempting to gain? Who do you want to meet? Take the initiative to create milestones and targets for yourself. Keep a log of your lessons learned.

- **Don't** be afraid to take initiative. If you see something that needs doing or a process that can be improved, don't hesitate to discuss it with your supervisor.

Résumé Development

I've seen this scenario unfold far too many times:

- A young woman puts herself out there and baits an opportunity.

- The bait is swallowed, and the request for a résumé is made.

- The young woman is startled by how quickly it all progresses but promises to send over her résumé the very next day.

- The next day arrives and she begins to tackle her résumé.

- Overwhelmed and a bit frustrated she thinks *He won't mind if it comes in tomorrow*, and she sits down to watch *Entertainment Tonight*.

- The next day arrives and she begins to tackle her résumé.

- Overwhelmed and a bit frustrated she thinks, *He won't mind if it comes in tomorrow*, and she sits down to watch *Entertainment Tonight*.

- A month later, the résumé is still not finished and the opportunity is lost.

While a résumé might not land you a job, not having a résumé can cost you one. The majority of jobs are discovered and secured within the context of a relationship, but your résumé is like the icing on the cake—a paper summary of your skills, experience, and qualifications. Keep the skeleton of your résumé updated at all times. You don't want to be scrambling to put your résumé together at the last minute, and then you can watch *Entertainment Tonight* guilt-free.

You could devote your entire career to résumé development, and there are hundreds of books, websites, and software programs out there to help you design an effective one. Don't get caught up in finding the perfect bullet point font. Instead, focus on making your résumé clear, concise, and most of all, error-free.

Here are some final résumé tips:

- Be prepared to focus your résumé on accomplishments by viewing your work as a project—with specific deliverables, outcomes, and results.

- Be prepared to fit your skills and abilities into the framework of the company you're pursuing. Don't just throw every single thing you've done onto the page and think, *Voilà! I'm done.* People hire (and pay for) what they need, what they want, and what they believe will save them time and money. Very specifically target your skills, experiences, and accomplishments to match the company you're applying to. Learn as much as you can beforehand and reflect the language, priorities, and values of the company.

Negotiation

The Quest for Success is filled with negotiation—with yourself and with others. As a Wildly Sophisticated woman you go after what you want, but unfortunately sometimes what *you* want is not what your boss, your boyfriend, or your co-worker wants. In these instances (and they will come up more often than you can imagine), you need to be prepared to negotiate. The ultimate goal of negotiation is to find the most profitable solution for both parties.

Self-respect is a question of recognizing that anything worth having has a price.
—Joan Didion

Before you even begin to tackle the logistical skills necessary for a successful negotiation, you have to *believe* you are worth it. A promotion, a raise, a new business deal—whatever your end goal, if you don't start with a full-fledged belief that you are worth it, you will not succeed.

Salary Negotiations

Carol Frohlinger is a managing partner in The Shadow Negotiation, LLC. (www.theshadownegotiation.com), a training company that focuses on helping women approach the bargaining table with confidence and come away with good results. Carol offers five tips and pieces of information for getting the salary you want:

- **Recognize negotiation is possible.** Almost everything is negotiable, but not unless you recognize the possibilities. Many women miss opportunities to negotiate and find the whole process stressful and distasteful. Even when they do recognize the opportunity, many will choose not to do it.

- **Early salaries serve as benchmarks.** You need to negotiate effectively even for your first job. Early salaries often become the benchmark for the future ones.

- **Package your skills.** Even if you are in a low leverage position, package your skills in a way that makes you stand out. The key is to match your skills to the priorities and needs of your employer. You can start by answering these questions:

- What knowledge, skills, and experience do you bring to the table?
- What results have you achieved that you can point to?
- Where do you think you may be vulnerable?
- What can you do to compensate for a lack of experience?

- **Identify both your alternatives and the other party's options.** When the other party senses that you have no alternative but to accept their offer, they will be tempted to give as little as possible, and you will be anxious to take it. Alternatives give you choices. Consider the question: *What will I do if we can't come to an agreement on the salary or responsibilities I want?*

- **Do your research.** The greatest tool in any negotiation is information. Make sure you know the fair market value for the job you are seeking, the salary range with a specific employer, and geographic, economic, industry, and company-specific factors that might affect the given salary. Also, try to obtain information on the employer's standard benefits package.

Here are some resources for determining your market value:

- Websites: www.salary.com
    www.jobstar.org
    www.monster.com
    www.hotjobs.com
    www.wetfeet.com
    www.vault.com

- People in your profession, last year's grads in your educational major, professional associations, and trade journals in your field.

- *The Occupational Outlook Handbook* (also available online at www.bls.gov/oco/home.htm).

One-on-One

You're on the Menu
Often, job interviews, negotiations, and business meetings will be held not in an office, but in a restaurant. If you're the focus of a business lunch meeting, I can guarantee you won't be eating much. Make sure you eat beforehand or have time scheduled to snack afterward. You only have to be stuck in one long, sleepy afternoon meeting with barely enough fuel to blink to remember this one!

What's Negotiable?
I'm with Carole. In my experience, almost everything is negotiable—it's just a matter of asking. You'd be surprised at how flexible your boss, your boyfriend, and even your landlord can be when you negotiate from a fair and well-informed position. Most people have only a handful of things they're unwilling to budge on. Figure out what these non-negotiables are and build your case from there. Understand what you really want and find ways that your company (or your negotiating partner) will actually "win" from the situation.

Creativity is the key. A client recently negotiated a "dry-cleaning" clause into her contract. With a travel schedule that would make you jet-lagged just thinking about it, one of her major challenges was having clean clothes to pack every Sunday night. She now has a deal whereby someone picks up her dry-cleaning on Friday evening and miraculously by Saturday at 4 P.M., her clothes are returned cleaned, pressed, and paid for.

Standard negotiable elements of a job offer include the following:

- **Salary**

- **Nonsalary compensation** Signing bonus, performance bonus, profit-sharing, deferred compensation, severance package, stock options

- **Relocation expenses** House-hunting, temporary living allowances, closing costs, travel expenses, spouse job-hunting/re-employment expenses

- **Benefits** Vacation days (number, amount paid, timing), personal days, sick days, insurance (medical, dental, vision, life, disability), automobile (or other transportation) allowance, professional training/conference attendance, continuing education (tuition reimbursement), professional memberships, club (country or athletic) memberships, product discounts, clothing allowance, short-term loans

- **Job specifics** Frequency of performance reviews, job title/role/duties, location/office, telecommuting, work hours and flexibility, starting date, performance standards/goals

✣   ✣   ✣

How are you feeling? Alarmed? Excited? Overwhelmed? It's all totally normal. Even as I write these preparation essentials, the little devil on my shoulder is whispering (whining, actually), This is so much work. Do I really have to do it all?

The answer to his question is yes—and no. At different points along your Quest, you will have different challenges and different work to do. I can almost guarantee you will never need to write a brand-new résumé, negotiate for a corner office, come to grips with your dream, and plan an internship in the same week. But if you do, fantastic!

This chapter provides the basic tools. Use them when you need them. Keep them in the back of your mind and do the work you need to do now. Preparing for success is a wonderful, worthwhile investment. Whatever your dreams or goals, preparation lays the groundwork and lets you fly without fear. It doesn't have to be tedious. Preparation is simply the best way to build confidence and excitement as you set out on your Quest.

6

Are You Willing to Accept Help?

Overcoming Isolation

It's one of those pivotal moments freeze-framed in my mind. I can still hear the traffic roar and see the sun splash across the glass office towers. In that moment, I "got it."

I was walking with my boss and mentor, Michael, to a big meeting with a group of potential investors. Michael was one of those people who has the guts to say what you need to hear and intuitively knows when you need to hear it. He believed in my abilities, and through constructive support and advice, taught me how to take my skills to the next level. As we approached the hotel lobby for our meeting, I was overcome with gratitude.

"Michael, I have to say, I don't know how I'm ever going to repay you for all your help. I've learned so much from you, and I'm incredibly thankful."

He stopped dead and turned to face me, his brows raised in surprise.

"Why are you thanking me, Nicole? Your enthusiasm and excitement has given me a whole new outlook on this business. Don't ever underestimate what you've given back."

I suddenly understood that help is a reciprocal process. I had felt so thankful for Michael's support and guidance that I didn't even consider what

I had offered him in return. In that moment, my entire outlook shifted. I begun to think about help as a gift—a chance to grow and to share the best of ourselves with another person.

As I began to build this chapter, I found reams of information about how to give help but very little about how to accept it. Clearly, we're a little uncomfortable with the topic. Although there are plenty of reasons why we feel driven to "do it ourselves," I'm here to tell you that accepting help is not a sign of weakness or a cop-out. Wildly Sophisticated women take responsibility for themselves, and part of that responsibility is knowing when and who to ask for help. It is an essential tool for creating success, not a sign of failure.

My flash of understanding with Michael taught me three crucial lessons about help:

- **Help will make you better.** Whether it's constructive criticism, fresh ideas, or good advice, you will go farther, faster with help from other people. Your Quest is unique, but the people who have gone before you have rich lessons to share.

- **Help is a two-way exchange.** This may be difficult to believe, but people want to help you. Your mentors and cheerleaders gain a very real sense of satisfaction from lighting your way. What's more, they will learn from both the process of helping you and from your unique blend of skills, opinions, and ideas. As a Wildly Sophisticated woman, you have much to offer.

- **Accepting help will enrich your Quest.** You simply can't do it alone—and you wouldn't want to. You are at the heart and the core of your Quest, but it is not a solitary pursuit. Some of the most exciting, satisfying, and absolutely thrilling parts of career development emerge when minds work together. Opportunities blossom when you open yourself to receive help.

You live an extremely busy life, and you have countless responsibilities. As you work to build career success, the pressure to be fully independent can leave even the best of us feeling isolated, stagnant, and ineffective. In order to achieve your true potential, you need to know how to overcome isolation and reach out to others. There is a lot to learn as you begin your Quest, but there will always be times when you need support and guidance. Learn how to accept help now, and you will benefit from this two-way exchange throughout your career.

This chapter has been broken down into four parts: Am I willing? Where do I find help? How do I ask for help? and What can I give back?

PART ONE
AM I WILLING?

It's funny—as I started to work through this chapter I dove immediately into the logistical aspects of accepting help—where to find it, how to ask for it, how to give it. Somewhere along the line I forgot the most important part of this success-building question: Am I willing? In conversations with women across the country (this sentence always means we're about to explore one of my own issues!), I've found that while we're more than willing to give help, we're much less likely to be willing to accept it. I suffer from my own willingness disease. Accepting help is hard. It can be attached to a price that's too high to pay and can create a sense of "owing" that changes the dynamic of our relationships.

I've only recently come to realize—and I know this sounds a little cheesy—that the willingness part is not tied to our heads but to our hearts.

> I was told to avoid the business altogether because of the rejection. People would say to me, "Don't you want to have a normal job and a normal family?" I guess that would be good advice for some people, but I wanted to act.
>
> —Jennifer Aniston

A willingness to accept help, at its core, requires feeling worthy, being prepared to give up a sense of control, and allowing ourselves to become vulnerable. Accepting help can be scary, but just like any fear, the better we can define what we're afraid of, the freer we become to surrender ourselves to the opportunities help can bring.

What's Stopping You?

Once you admit you need help, a world of opportunity and support opens up to you. It all starts with the question, "Am I willing?" Even if your answer is no, identifying why you're not ready or able to receive assistance will move you closer to the point of graceful acceptance. Take a read through the following common fears about accepting help and see if any sound familiar to you.

Criticism

"Your idea sucks. You should have approached the project from a different angle. Don't quit your day job." Is there anything more distressing than putting yourself out there, only to be shot down?

As we set out on the Quest, the last thing we want to hear is that we're not doing it right, that we're on the wrong path, or that our dreams are unthinkable. I remember the day I was asked the question, "Who Do You Think You Are?" I felt criticized. I was looking for help and direction, and I wasn't prepared for what I got in return.

Criticism can make us defensive and protective and prevent us from accessing the help we need. I've come to learn that you can use criticism to your advantage. Not everyone is going to like your style, your work, or your idea, but don't let criticism deflate you. In fact, you can use it to give you strength and determination.

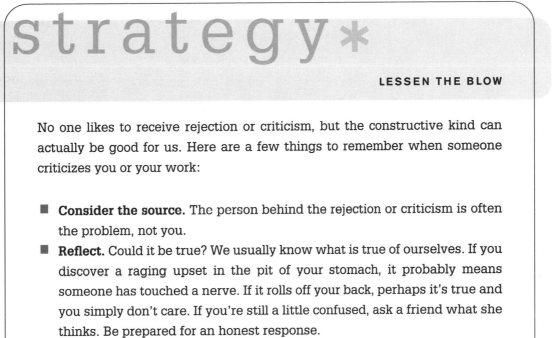

strategy*

LESSEN THE BLOW

No one likes to receive rejection or criticism, but the constructive kind can actually be good for us. Here are a few things to remember when someone criticizes you or your work:

- **Consider the source.** The person behind the rejection or criticism is often the problem, not you.
- **Reflect.** Could it be true? We usually know what is true of ourselves. If you discover a raging upset in the pit of your stomach, it probably means someone has touched a nerve. If it rolls off your back, perhaps it's true and you simply don't care. If you're still a little confused, ask a friend what she thinks. Be prepared for an honest response.
- **Make a decision.** What do you want to do about it? Is this an attribute, skill, or personality trait you would like to improve? If your presentation skills have been criticized, can you take a refresher course or spend some time upgrading your expertise?

You Ask, but You Don't Receive

It takes guts and vulnerability to ask for help. What happens if you ask, and the person on the other end says no? Sometimes it takes so long to psych ourselves up enough to ask that we put way too much value on the response. This is a time to play "What if?" What if someone says no? Then ask someone else. Realize ahead of time that you might not get the help you need the very first time you ask. Have patience and use each request to build your confidence. It does get easier.

Career Confession

UNLIKELY MOTIVATION

I've drawn inspiration from the most unlikely sources. As a twenty-six-year-old actor starting a handbag business, I knew it was going to be tough. But surprisingly, I've started to feel more confident after hearing the odds are against me rather than words of encouragement. I've started to run on adrenaline attached to the dream of saying "I told you so!"

When I first started my company, I met with a consultant to ask her about what type of business license I should get. I was feeling unusually timid when I walked into her office. I couldn't help thinking—a handbag business? The *last thing* the world needs are more handbags. Perhaps reading my mind, she started by telling me, "The odds of succeeding with a small business are the same as winning the lottery"—fighting words that I guess I needed to hear. For the rest of the meeting I was completely fired up. Suddenly I felt like I was back in high school, listening to AC/DC's "Thunderstruck" right before a big basketball game.

Sometimes I think it's twisted to feel encouraged by my chances of failure, but then I realize that the odds will always beat you if you let them.

Nina, entrepreneur

The Price Is Too Steep

At some point in our lives, we've all had this experience. In the mall, the car dealership, wherever . . . we ask for something simple and we get some guy breathing down our neck. "Yeah, baby. I'll help you find that wrench set . . . if you'll give me your phone number . . ."

Umm, no thanks. I'll find it myself.

This is a case where the "help" is simply not worth it. At points along your Quest, you might find yourself in a more professional version of this little scenario (it's called sexual harassment). Don't let this fear stop you from asking for help, but know your boundaries ahead of time. If the price is too steep, walk away. There will always be someone out there who's happy to help—no strings attached.

You Don't Want to Show Weakness

Call it pride or insecurity, but fear of looking less than perfect is extremely common. Relax. No one is judging you as harshly as you judge yourself. Asking for help is infinitely better than getting yourself in an even bigger mess by stumbling through on your own. No one's perfect, and no one expects you to be.

Death Grip

"Sure, I'd love to invest in your business. I'll sign the check . . . after you drop off the business plan, meet with my accountant, and hire my designers to revamp your website. Then we can spend next week re-structuring my filing system." Have you ever been in this situation?

Help is a two-way street, and once we accept help, we often worry there's an unspoken (or totally overt) commitment to play by someone else's rules. Avoid this trap. Before you accept help, make sure your boundaries are clearly defined. In order to fully live your Quest, you need the autonomy to make your own choices and do things your way. People will help and contribute in ways you never may have expected, but you have to ensure you are still in the driver's seat.

What Kind of Help Are You Looking For?

All help is not created equal. What's the difference? Bad help makes you feel guilty, and it often comes back to haunt you. Maybe you're even compromising

Career Confession
DINNERTIME CATHARSIS

I was so nervous, I couldn't even eat. I was having dinner with my parents, and we were about to have The Talk. No—not that one. I think my mom first pulled out those uterus diagrams fifteen years ago.

I was about to ask for help. Actually, I was about to ask if I could move back home for a few months—just until I could get back on my feet, financially speaking. Trust me, it was the last thing I wanted, but at the time, it was my only option.

I've always prided myself on my independence. I like to—no, I must—succeed at everything I do, on my own terms. Maybe I still don't understand the idea of unconditional love, but I thought that if I admitted I needed help, they would think I was a failure. Still, I took a deep breath, turned ghostly white, and asked.

Luckily (though not surprisingly), my parents were totally supportive and helped me see that my financial problems were temporary. We worked out an arrangement that we could all live with, and it felt amazing to finally unload all that stress and anxiety. Their support meant the world to me. But even better, I realized that by accepting help, I was now better equipped to take action. I was still in charge.

Angie, teacher

yourself or making a trade-off that isn't worth the end result. Bad help simply feels wrong. On the flip side, good help makes you feel empowered and abundant. Once you relinquish control, you feel relieved. The support actually enriches your experience and gives you the strength to go further faster.

It's no surprise to hear that help comes in many different forms—and that all help is not created equal. It's another thing entirely to put this little adage into action. Before you ask for assistance, you must know exactly what you need. Otherwise, it's kind of like asking your boyfriend if that new pair of pants makes you look fat. You don't want a critic. You're looking for positive reinforcement (if only men could learn this simple lesson). This also highlights the importance of asking the right person. While your boyfriend stammers, tongue-tied and scared to respond, your best friend knows exactly what to say. Use the following profiles to identify who can offer the help you really need.

- **The cheerleader.** Perky, positive, and over-the-top enthusiastic, the cheerleader offers unconditional support. No matter how disheartened you feel, she lifts your spirits, takes you out for martinis, and generally thinks you're fabulous. Pragmatism, be damned. Never underestimate the power of someone screaming your name from the sidelines.

- **The taskmaster.** You've got some serious work to do, but your ass has developed a magnetic attraction to the couch. You need someone to crack the whip, and that person is the taskmaster. Maybe she gives you ultimatums (no girls' night until you finish that report) or hounds you with questions (when *will* I read your screenplay?)—her actual techniques are irrelevant. What's important is that she's a total pain in the ass and as much as you hate it, she gets you moving.

- **The teacher.** Buried under a mountain of books, files, and illegible Post-it notes, you realize, "I still don't have a clue." You need a teacher. She's the bright spark in your field who will show you exactly how to cross the Ts and dot the Is. Don't expect her to hold your hand, but do take advantage of her Yoda-like wisdom.

- **The connector.** You have explicit fantasies about flipping through her Rolodex. In reality, she's moved well beyond mere paper, honey. You would need less training to fly an airplane than to navigate her Palm Pilot. The connector can hook you up with anyone, anywhere. Even better, these people can actually help you. She's spent years nurturing an enviable circle of resources and allies, so use your connector wisely (and treat her extremely well). Inside her high-tech toys lies a career building gold mine.

- **The muse.** After an early morning coffee with the muse, you're going to re-paint your apartment, find spiritual fulfillment, and build a fashion empire to rival Kate Spade—today. It's partly the caffeine talking, but her amazing blend of poise and determination fuels your inner fires and pushes your creativity into a whole new time zone. If you find yourself in a rut, go seek out the muse.

Help Yourself

I've met two kinds of clients in my career management practice: those who are willing to help themselves and those who aren't. It's pretty easy to tell the difference. One woman comes to our second meeting with a list of calls made, research completed, and a new sense of focus. The other arrives late, expecting me to have reformatted her résumé and set up an important meeting. This isn't about being able to do it all on your own—it is the sense of responsibility in making others' help and guidance work for you. It's the willingness, and especially the initiative, to take the necessary steps on your own. Someone can guide you, but you have to pick up the phone and do the groundwork. Your helper will be one hundred times more willing and effective if you take responsibility for yourself and your goals.

> I read and walked for miles at night along the beach . . . searching endlessly for someone wonderful who would step out of the darkness and change my life. It never crossed my mind that that person could be me.
> —Anna Quindlen

PART TWO
WHERE DO I FIND HELP?

I think my long-time friend had said it about one hundred times.

"Nic, you need to have patience with building this business. Yes, you need to work hard, but you also have to realize it's gonna take time."

I'd always nod my head feigning agreement, thinking to myself, *Whatever.*

Then a few weeks ago I met with a successful woman who had built her consulting business with tooth-and-nail determination. She was inspiring. She was experienced. She was delightful. And when I asked for her best piece of advice, she looked me in the eyes and said, "You need to have faith that it will all come together. It takes time. You need to have patience."

A smile lit up my face. This woman is brilliant! What wonderful advice!

Later that night, my friend and I met for drinks. I excitedly told her about my day and relayed the story of my inspiring meeting. When I got to the part about patience, she shot me the "you've got to be kidding me" look. I shut up.

If you're anything like most of the young women I know, the down-and-dirty professional help you need can't come from your Aunt Linda or your friend Karen (and even if it does, sometimes it's easier to accept from someone *not* intimately tied to your personal life). It's infinitely more helpful to access professional advice from someone who's acquainted with your industry and has expertise you can learn from. The question is—where to find this help? This section explores how to develop and maintain a personal support network, the ins and outs of mentorship, and the often-overlooked lessons you can learn from your boss.

> **After *The Matrix*, I can't wear sunglasses. As soon as I put them on, people recognize me.**
>
> —Carrie-Anne Moss

Career Confession

"Guess what, Mom? I made a new friend today!"

My giddy enthusiasm might make you think of a sloppy six-year-old. But I'm a twenty-five-year-old gal, living in the Big City, who has embarked upon a search far more significant than finding the perfect male companion: I am trying to make friends.

Girlfriends, that is. At this point in my young adult life, I have geographically moved away from my high school friends, and my college friends have scattered across the globe or married and unplugged their phones. I find myself home alone too often, and I'm looking for a new set of gals to roam the city streets (and bars) with: My very own estrogen-powered urban gang.

Actually cultivating the new friendship is the hard part. You have to be persistent but not creepy. You have to sound vibrant but not flighty. After all, you shouldn't scare the poor dear away (given my track record, I tend to save that for the guys). The best thing to do is give her a ring, leave a message, and wait for the callback—at which point my neurosis really kicks in.

I absolutely convince myself that she will never call me and that she finds me to be lame, pushy, or even worse: desperate. This, of course, is completely not true, and she is most likely thrilled to receive a call from a prospective new gal pal. The reality is that making friends is essential to being happy in a city full of young go-getters, most of whom are from out of town. Friends (especially girlfriends, given our attentive nature) serve as a surrogate family during the holidays, help out when you're sick, and forbid you to walk out in *those* pants.

I recall checking my messages while walking downtown one day and listening to my first callback from a new girlfriend. My excitement at hearing her message and invitation for coffee paralleled the satisfaction of knowing that hot guy from the night before actually made use of my number. Who knows? Maybe he'll even be able to introduce me to a few good women . . .

Solana, investment banker

> ### One-on-One
>
> *The Octopus*
>
> You meet by the complimentary bar, and once you've introduced yourself, bam! She's got her tentacles wrapped all around you. At parties, professional functions, or networking events—we've all met the octopus. She's a little nervous and extremely uncomfortable meeting new people, so she clings to anyone who seems nonthreatening. Her reaction is normal. Many young women feel anxious in unfamiliar situations, and a friendly face can make all the difference. But you'll both gain more from the experience if you circulate and join different conversations. Politely but firmly, untangle her tentacles and introduce the octopus to someone else. Then run, don't walk, to the other side of the room!

Networking

It's like a junior high school dance. You're in a darkened gymnasium (conference room) with a glass of punch (wine) in your hand. The boys (men) are on one side laughing and smacking each other (talking sports) while the girls (women) are on the other side, comparing shoes and lipstick (comparing shoes). So many "networking" events are just like that dance—they're rigid, they're lonely, and they don't really get going until someone spikes the punch.

Trust me, I hate those bad wine and soggy cheese events as much as you do, so Wildly Sophisticated Media created Drinks After Work. When young women came together to share their Career Confessions and offer ideas for this book, we were amazed at the lively, spontaneous, and natural connections that sprang up over coffee. We were also surprised when these busy young women would call and e-mail to ask, "When's the next meeting?" Had we just held a networking event? Almost accidentally, we realized that young women were hungry for honest conversations without the name-tag bullshit.

With Drinks After Work, we are redefining the word *networking* and building a safe place for women to come together and share both their challenges and their triumphs. Think Friday night cocktails and a rundown of your workweek—or not. We want to get women connecting and laughing through the Quest with each other. At the end of this book, you'll find more information about Drinks After Work.

So forget about collecting business cards. Wherever you are, try to connect with three intriguing people, rather than doing the standard meet and greet with twenty-three. Make it fun, make it relaxed, and do step out on that dance floor.

Mentorship

Put yourself in someone else's shoes for a moment.

A young, lovely woman approaches you nervously. She arranges a meeting and with shining eyes, full of hope, looks across your desk and asks, "Will you be my mentor?"

You swallow hard and resist the urge to pull the fire alarm. Your mind races. You distract her with candy and think as fast as you can. *Okay. Mentor. Mentor. That means I have to shape her career, introduce her to everyone I have ever known and met, and take full responsibility for her personal and professional development.*

You pretend to choke on your coffee stalling for a few more seconds. Her wide eyes blink longingly. *Will there be a ceremony?* you wonder. *A baptismal gown and water? Do I even have a wing, and is it big enough to fit another person underneath?* Decision time. How would you respond to this sweet young woman in your office?

"Hell, no!"

The term *mentor* has become infused with as much meaning and responsibility as the word *godparent*. It insinuates a lifetime of commitment and a higher spiritual plane. In reality, your garbage man could become your mentor. With sage advice about life, love, and low-risk investments, he could be just the person you were looking for. It's time to re-define the word *mentor*. A mentor is anyone who helps and nurtures your Quest. She's a more experienced person who is willing to

> ## One-on-One
>
> ### *Be Careful What You Wish For*
>
> **You've painstakingly created a portfolio of your architectural projects. Fresh out of school, you've hit the jackpot. You've found a mentor. She has connections and an amazing career of her own, and your head is practically bursting with excitement. This is someone who can really help you! The first meeting arrives. She reviews your portfolio and says you have great promise, but your skills aren't up to industry standards. She suggests some computer drafting courses and tells you to call if you need any more help. As you leave her office, you resist the overwhelming urge to throw your portfolio in the Dumpster. The last thing you want to do is take more classes . . .**
>
> **Accepting help or advice from a mentor isn't always easy. You're usually still learning, and it can make you feel vulnerable. Just remember that your mentor isn't always a cheerleader *or* a critic. She's someone who has your best professional interests in mind and is working to help you succeed. To truly benefit from a mentorship relationship, and if you really want to grow, you have to embrace constructive evaluations. Don't get defensive.**

share her resources, knowledge, and encouragement. Your mentor has the background information and insider expertise in an area in which you are looking to grow and learn. Her only prerequisite is to treat you with respect and authenticity.

No wings, no gowns, no contracts written in blood.

Where Do I Find a Mentor?

I can remember the day distinctly, and what I can tell you for sure is that after meeting my new next-door neighbor, I never, ever dreamed he would become my mentor. I don't know what it is, but we somehow think our mentors should wear small badges indicating their status and live in guarded ivory towers. The reality is, mentors are everywhere—at the Y, down the street, in the grocery store. Finding a mentor is not always a major, strategic undertaking. More often that not, they're right under your nose.

Sometimes a mentor just falls into your life, and at other times you go searching for one. Some mentors stay with you throughout your career, and others only penetrate your life for a short period of time or help you through a specific challenge. Regardless of the situation, the one thing you always need to have is a clear focus and intention. What do you want to learn from this person and process? If you determine what you want from a mentor before you go looking for one, you'll make a much more constructive connection and you'll gain far more from the experience. And while some employers offer formal mentoring programs, don't wait for a mentor to come to you—go out and find one who fits your needs.

What Are My Responsibilities to My Mentor?

The best mentorship relationships have a reciprocal, almost karmalike dimension. Don't underestimate your role in helping to facilitate and support this relationship.

- **Keep your mentor in the loop.** Mentors, just like all of us, want to know that their assistance made a difference. Whether your mentor has helped you set up a meeting or suggested a reading list, keep her in the loop. Write her a quick note thanking her for the reading material suggestions and let her know what you learned. E-mail her an update about the outcome of the meeting she helped arrange. People enjoy helping, especially if they can see results.

- **Play by the rules.** Do not embarrass your mentor with your behavior. Prepare for your meeting. Dress appropriately. Show up on time. Your goal is to have the person you are meeting with call your mentor and thank them for the introduction to you.

- **Show your appreciation.** Thank you, thank you, and thank you again. No one likes to feel taken advantage of, least of all a busy, successful professional who is offering you support, information, and introductions.

- **Share your Wildly Sophisticated attitude.** You might not always feel like it, but you have a tremendous amount to offer as a mentee. Your fresh and energetic perspective, your commitment to excellence, and your willingness to learn are all amazing gifts you can offer your mentor. Ask questions, learn more about the work your mentor is involved with, and explore ways in which you can offer her support.

Your Boss

Someone very early in my career suggested, "Don't choose a job; choose your boss." I've come to learn that they were right—don't underestimate how important your bosses can be to your career.

I know what you're thinking: *I just found a job I love, and now you want me to hand-pick my boss?* Just trust me on this one. A great boss can provide you with career-long support and direction. It's well worth the investment.

So is your boss your mentor? The million-dollar question. In my experience, it's hard to talk freely about your desire to explore other career options with the boss who loves your work and is somehow expecting that, at twenty-six years old, you will one day be retiring with the firm. In my experience, although your boss might offer many of the same supports as a mentor, there is an important distinction. Generally speaking, your boss wants to support your "job" development—your rise within the ranks of your current organization—whereas your mentor has a more objective perspective on your career as a whole and is less tied to any specific outcome.

That being said, ex-bosses can make great mentors. Not only do they intimately understand your work style, skills, and abilities, if you've honed a respect-based relationship that you've exited professionally, many bosses will feel personally invested in your success for the long haul.

Both current and ex-bosses provide important references and contacts in your industry. Taking the time to find a first-rate boss will pay off in the long

Career Confession

MAKE IT STOP

Why does this elevator stop at every floor? I mis-timed my lunch break, and now I'm on the most excruciating thirty-floor ride of my life. My boss is someone who, how shall I put it, loves to "overshare." Starting out in my career I really wanted to believe that my boss would be someone I could look up to and emulate. I've got a dud. From office gossip to "too much information," I'm now fully up to date on her husband's latest Viagra status.

The worst part is that she truly expects me to care. If I don't show enough fake sympathy for her ridiculous problems she'll pass me over again for a promotion. It's like kindergarten class, and now I'm twenty-eight floors away from either a gold star or a trip to the corner.

Kim, hotel administrator

---

run because she can offer support and long-term mentorship, and if she's a front-runner in her field, she may be able to "bring you along" as she advances through your industry. But repeat after me: *My boss is not my parent* or *my friend*. Say it again.

"You Remind Me of Myself"

Consider these words music to your ears. One of the best things that can happen along your Quest for Success is to have your boss claim to see herself in you. What do these words actually mean? If managed correctly, it means you will be taken under her wing, and she will offer special attention in her efforts to support you and your career. She will watch out for you and have a sense of loyalty around the creation of your success. But be careful. These words also mean you better not disappoint her—she'll be extra pissed off watching "herself" making a mistake.

Even if you're not her Mini-Me, a great boss makes all the difference in the world. I've had both amazing bosses and shitty bosses throughout my career, and I didn't necessarily know what I was in for from the get-go. In reality, your boss will reveal her most important attributes slowly, over the course of your relationship. It's sort of hard to ask in an interview, "Okay, so you say you want me to succeed, but will you steal my ideas and hog the glory?" Maybe you can't be quite this frank, but don't hesitate to ask your prospective employer about her management style and request the opportunity to speak with other employees.

Interestingly, much of what you believe makes a great boss is directly tied to what you know about yourself. Review Who You Think You Are. A great boss for one person might not be the best boss for another. It all depends on your learning style, what inspires you, and what you want from the relationship and your workplace.

Despite individual differences, there are some common characteristics that help make a great boss:

- **She knows when to support and when to push.** Great bosses are both cheerleaders and constructive critics. They know when you need reassurance and support, and they know when to push you to your capacity. This is a great issue to explore with other employees. Ask questions like "How do you feel challenged by your boss? Do you feel supported?"

- **She's an effective leader.** A great leader is someone who shares responsibility appropriately, doesn't burden you beyond your capacity, can delegate effectively, and gives you proper credit for your work. Her behavior toward you doesn't fluctuate with her moods. Ask your potential boss some questions: "What's your leadership style? Whose leadership style do you admire? Do you participate on boards or professional organizations, either within the company or industry? Who has led you in your career?"

- **You can learn from her.** The foundation-building years of our career are filled with intensive learning. Your boss should be someone who down-right enjoys sharing her knowledge. This is a great topic to explore with your potential boss in an interview. When asked if you have any questions, feel free to ask about her teaching style.

- **She's inspiring.** She's someone you can look up to—someone who is challenging herself and scaling her own personal and professional mountains. Inspiration is a topic to explore both with other employees and with your potential new boss. Bosses have lives outside of work, too, and one of the quickest routes to learn a little more about her passion is to ask her what she finds inspiring. If this line of questioning feels too personal or is obviously inappropriate, you can also find some signs in her office—pictures of family, quotes on the wall, books on her bookshelf.

One-on-One

Who's the Boss?

You might have noticed I'm using the term *boss* the way many teenagers say the word *like*. There's a method to my madness. Whether you work in an office, at a newspaper, or even for yourself, everyone has bosses. They're the people you're accountable to: investors, editors, supervisors, coaches, professors, clients, and mentors. A boss by any other name is still a boss!

PART THREE
HOW DO I ASK FOR HELP?

You won't get help if you don't ask for it. Or as hockey legend Wayne Gretzky said, "You miss 100 percent of the shots you never take." It seems simple, but asking for help requires preparation and an ability to articulate your needs. It's a skill you can develop with time. Here are some hints for effectively seeking help:

- **Find the right time.** Do not, I repeat, do not approach your boss for a raise right after that three-day round of budget meetings. She just spent hours slashing costs and hunting for ways to save a dime. It might sound obvious, but when it comes to asking for help, timing is everything.

- **Be precise.** No one can read your mind. If you are asking your boss for help with a particularly challenging assignment, indicate what you have done to date. Emphasize that you are not asking her to solve your problem but to support you with suggestions, ideas, or input. If you approach people with specific, measurable requests, it's far easier for them to respond—and they'll be better equipped to help.

- **Ask authentically.** It's all about that Wildly Sophisticated attitude. Your body language, posture, even your word choices will influence how others respond. Believe in your request and emphasize the big picture. People will be much more eager to help if they feel you're building and creating something you feel passionate about (even if it's just your résumé right now).

strategy*

At some point on your Quest, asking for help will require you to contact a stranger or a new acquaintance—the cold call. Your first call may be a little nerve-racking, but relax. Cold calling gets easier with practice. It's a highly valuable skill to add to your repertoire, so take a deep breath and pick up the phone.

The following tips can help you make the call with confidence and finesse:

- **Say your full name.**
  "Hi Nicole, this is Karen White."

- **State the organization you are with or what you do.**
  "I work for National Media, a New York firm that specializes in promoting authors."

- **Provide some context.** This will help them remember how they know you, or if you haven't met, take a second to introduce yourself.
  "We met briefly in New York when John Howe introduced us," or *"John Howe suggested I give you a call."*

- **State why you are calling.**
  "I'm calling to introduce you to our company's services and to learn more about your needs for your upcoming book release."

- **Assume the person may be busy.**
  "Do you have a few minutes? Is this a good time to talk?"

- **Offer to reschedule.** If it's not a good moment, ask if you could schedule a more convenient time or send an e-mail.
  "Nicole, I would love to learn more about your needs. Is there a time this week when we could schedule some time to talk?" *"I can see this isn't the best time for you. How about if I send you an e-mail outlining our services and follow up in a few days? What is your e-mail address?"*

- **Ask *before* you hit bottom.** You really don't want to be slinking in the door Monday morning, knowing you can't possibly meet that 11 A.M. deadline. If you feel like you're groping for answers, ask before the crunch time hits. Your boss might have happily given you an extension if you had only asked last Tuesday.

- **Be prepared to hear "no."** Let's face it—people are not puppets (even when that would make life easier!). Know that when you ask for help, the other person might not have the time, the energy, or even the desire to help. Don't take it personally, and above all else, don't let one "no" (or two or three or fifteen) stop you from asking someone else.

- **Offer something in return.** I'd like to tell you that people always love to help simply for the sake of helping, but the reality is that helping has a reciprocal nature. People keenly remember when someone goes out of their way to assist or encourage them and will want to return the favor. More than simple give and take, being generous to others polishes your own karma. The world (and other people) will gladly offer helping hands.

PART FOUR
WHAT CAN I GIVE BACK?

One of my favorite memories is running my very first race and feeling the energy of the crowds cheering on the sidelines. I wasn't expecting that foreign faces lining the streets of the route and shouts of "You can do it!" would have any real impact on my energy level (they weren't there for me), but they did. I learned that one of the best things we have to give others doesn't cost a dime: It's our energy, our good wishes, our cheers of hope and support. Help has this wonderfully reciprocal nature, and celebrating someone else's contributions inspires us to give our best to the world around us.

A Token of Your Appreciation

At a busy networking event during the height of the Internet boom, I met a high-powered, well-respected investor. After an evening filled with stimulating conversation and an offer to provide some professional guidance on a project I was working on, I immediately added my new contact to the top of my database. The next day, I sent a quick e-mail of thanks and a great article relevant to our conversation. A day later, I had a message on my voicemail. "If you ever need financing for any of the projects you are working on, give me a call." A few years later, after the Internet bust, I took him up on his offer. Little gestures go a long way.

Here are a few other low- and no-cost gifts to express your appreciation and make those little gestures:

- Heartfelt thank you letters

- An offer to take someone out for coffee

- An interesting article, news clipping, or a useful web link

- Photos of you together (appropriate only within a close relationship . . . and of course, only if the photo makes you look particularly stunning)

- Gift certificates

- Flowers

Take Initiative

Your boss is under a deadline. She has been at the office twelve hours a day for fourteen days straight. Clearly, she needs your help but is too busy to ask for it.

As you prepare to go home at 9 P.M., you notice her light is still on. You approach her office and knock lightly on the open door. Her red eyes greet you and, like an angel, you ask, "What can I do to help you?"

At first, your question is music to her ears. She thinks to herself, *Could it be possible? Could someone actually help with this mess?* And then, suddenly, you see her expression drop from elation to distress as she remembers the last time she actually accepted help—and found disappointment. Alas, she ended up having to do the work all over again.

> I want people to be blown away when I do what they don't expect.
> —Drew Barrymore

Do you want to make an impact on your boss? Do you want to be promoted? Do you want to get a raise? Do you want to become invaluable? Do you want to contribute? If you answered yes to any of these questions, think like a Wildly Sophisticated woman. Don't ask your boss what you can contribute; ask yourself what you can contribute. Wildly Sophisticated women take the initiative and find ways to help others. It's not about martyrdom; rather, it's an important way to create your own success.

Underpromise and Overdeliver

Caroline was all smiles as we shook hands. I left the bank feeling great—here was this young, dynamic woman who was going to consolidate my debt and give us a fantastic new mortgage rate. I hadn't planned to switch banks, but Caroline had wooed me with her enthusiasm and, of course, the numbers to back it up.

A week later, I went in to sign some papers and Caroline wasn't quite so chipper. All her promises had fallen through. In fact, the whole package was

strategy*

To really excel at this strategy, you need to understand two critical realities. One: Most managers are not great at delegating. They talk about delegation but actually have difficulty relinquishing control. Two: Your boss has asked before and been disappointed with the result. You are going to have to take the initiative and earn her trust.

- **Start with observation.** What is your boss struggling with? If she has not told you directly or asked for help, look for signs. They're everywhere. You also want to have a firm grasp on your boss's standards for her own work. How does she work? What is her communication style? How does she like to have material presented to her?
- **Take small pieces.** This is important for two reasons. One: You don't want to dive into a big part of the work and then find you are going down the wrong path because you've done a lot of guesswork. Two: Your boss is not going to hand over everything at once. Prove you can be trusted in small increments. Do a small job extremely well, rather than a large job haphazardly. Quality, not quantity, is the key to this strategy.
- **Approach your boss with your contribution.** You might want to say, "I can see you are working on landing this new client. I spent some time over the weekend doing some research. Can this help?"
- **Follow up.** In all likelihood, you will have knocked your boss's socks off and she will be sure to let you know how much she appreciated your contribution. If not, check in to see if there is anything you could have done differently.

worse than what I had at my old bank. All I gained was a headache—and a personal reminder of a critical lesson. Repeat after me: Underpromise. Overdeliver.

I've seen countless young women who are so eager to please, they promise to do things they either can't do or don't know if they can actually complete. They take on huge, challenging tasks and underestimate the time and effort involved: "Write up the meeting minutes by tomorrow? Sure! Why don't I also turn them into a newsletter, post them on the company website, and arrange next month's meeting?" Don't put yourself in this situation. No one will think less of you for being realistic. If anything, promise to complete the absolute minimum possible, then give it your maximum effort. When you not only meet but exceed people's expectations, you will truly keep them happy.

✺ ✺ ✺

I'm guilty of being a half-ass acceptor of help.

Sure, I'll accept help, but I'll expect it won't be done the way I wanted or to be wracked with guilt. That's not willingness. And until you are willing, the help you need will not appear.

Expectations are directly tied to outcomes. If you think you'll get shitty help, you will. On the other hand, when you can get over yourself enough to simply make the request—to the universe, to your friends, to strangers—the floodgates open and you start to receive amazing gifts. Willingness comes from your heart, not your head. Before you decide I've inhaled a little too much incense, think about it this way: Someone could give you the most kick-ass advice in the world, but if you're not willing to consider or accept their help, it might as well be a dirty handshake. When you're not ready for help, you'll just sabotage it in the end, anyway.

Here's the best part: You don't have to be ready, just be honest with yourself. There's no shame in admitting you're not prepared to accept someone else's help. I'm guessing it's like having a baby. You know one day you'll have to send your grown child out into the world. But while that baby's still in dia-

pers, no way. You'll do whatever you need to ensure she's protected. It's great to realize you'll only waste your time and someone else's when you ask for help you're not willing to actually embrace.

As I look back over this chapter, its outcome reinforces for me that if you want your experience, your work, and your life to be enriched, asking for help is a pivotal part of the Quest for Success.

7

Are You Ready to Give
This Everything You've Got?

Living with Imbalance

To-Do List:

Pick up dry cleaning

Get hair highlighted

Explore spiritual fulfillment

Meet with investors

Call grandparents

Fight aging

Let's be honest. Balance is one of those words like *happiness* or *fulfillment* that makes us feel like, "Oh yeah, I'll get on it. Right after I do my taxes, walk the dog, and organize my desk." Of all the Wildly Sophisticated women I've interviewed, not one of them describes their life as balanced. *Balance* is a word that conjures up feelings of guilt—thoughts of *I haven't been to the gym in three weeks, I really should do my laundry* and the all too familiar defense response, *What's wrong with take-out four nights a week?*

While a well-rounded life is critical for sustaining a healthy personal and

> **Keep working hard and you can get anything you want. But don't think it's going to be easy. It's hard!**
>
> —Aaliyah

professional life, striving for success oftentimes requires imbalance. The Quest for Success is not always a smooth or direct journey. There are some junctures that require a high level of focus and commitment, and re-prioritizing our lives becomes sheer necessity. Whether you're taking on a new assignment, deciding to travel, writing a screenplay, having a baby, going back to school, or competing in an Ironman, there will be moments that will require you to ask yourself, "Am I Ready to Give This Everything I've Got?"

There is a critical step between deciding on your goals and bringing them to life. It's at this exact juncture where you have to ask yourself, "Am I Willing to Give This Everything I've Got?" Perseverance, discipline, and commitment are the keys to bringing your dreams to life. The more consciously you decide you are up for the challenge, the more likely you are to succeed.

The four C's—commitment, control, choice vs. compromise, and completion—are the focus of this chapter.

PART ONE
COMMITMENT

It's crystal clear outside. You know, the kind of day that beckons you to join it—challenging you to stay inside, away from its freshness and life. It feels somewhat fitting that as I look out the window at this beautiful day, imagining a lingering, window-shopping stroll down Madison Avenue, running in the park, even digging into that neglected garden (funny how anything seems more appealing when challenged with a dreaded task), I'm committed to write about commitment.

There is a price to pay for success, and it usually comes in the form of commitment. There are going to be a hundred things you'd rather do than save money, study for your securities exam, or actually write the novel that's swimming around in your head. The reality is, if you want to experience achievement, you have to commit to the work it takes to get you there. In my experience, commitment is the difference between mediocrity and excellence. Here are some tried-and-true principles of commitment.

The Wildly Sophisticated Principles of Commitment

When the Going Gets Tough . . . Remind Yourself of Your Purpose
It's not always going to be easy. In fact, it will sometimes be hard, but by focusing on the purpose behind your commitment you will be able to do what is necessary to persevere. The pleasure, joy, and/or desire attached to your purpose should exceed the pain. In times of hardship, when you feel tempted to give up, remind yourself why you are committed in the first place. *Note:* There are going to be days when you will answer "No, quite frankly, the pleasure doesn't outweigh the pain." But before you throw in the towel, sleep on it—you might feel differently in the morning.

- If your commitment level is wavering, re-assess your commitment. Why did you commit in the first place? Does the purpose behind your commitment still make sense to you?

Commitment Builds Commitment
If you have been labeled a commitment-phobic, here's some great news: With practice you can strengthen your ability to commit. If you are considering a large commitment—saving for a new home—start small and build your confidence in incremental steps. For one week, commit to making your own coffee, then the following week, commit to packing your own lunch. Commitment has a special kind of reward system. Accomplishment, combined with commitment,

grows confidence. By the end of the month, you will feel ready and able to make the 100 percent commitment plunge.

- Is there a companion commitment you can make that, while different, will sustain your momentum, discipline, and excitement for your primary goal?

Quantify Your Commitment

I'm sure you have met those people who talk a lot about commitment but never actually follow through. I worked with a young client who told me up, down, and sideways that she was committed to acing the LSAT. After weeks of frustration and limited improvement on her practice test scores, I challenged her to quantify her commitment—to actually record how many hours she studied each week. Her guess without actually recording her commitment was twelve hours a week. The reality? Four.

- If you feel committed but aren't seeing the outcome you expected, consider quantifying your commitment. You might be surprised.

Think About Your Whole Life

Commitment requires compromise and the ability to focus. As you take on a commitment, consider how it will affect other aspects of your life. Most of us have more than one commitment in our lives. You need to think about how your new commitment to a promotion affects your commitment to exercise, your commitment to your boyfriend, and your commitment to volunteer at the YWCA. You can set yourself up for success by prioritizing your commitments and eliminating the clutter in your life. You might have to make concessions, engage in hard conversations, and create boundaries around the rest of your life in order to set yourself up for success.

> **Instant gratification is not soon enough.**
> —Meryl Streep

- Clutter might come in the form of negative thoughts about yourself, a messy closet, or a relationship that lacks closure. How can you eliminate the clutter in your life?

Reward Yourself

So I did it. On that bright, glorious day, I resisted the temptation to sprint out into the sunshine, and I finished writing this piece on commitment. What's next? Well, I'm a firm believer you need to feed your commitment, and I'm hungry for a new Coach bag.

- Make sure that after you've seen through your commitment, you reward yourself with some pleasure!

strategy*

THE POWER OF COMMITMENT

There are going to be some challenging situations and circumstances that will predictably exhaust your patience and require a level of commitment you didn't know you had. Identify an experience in which you were absolutely committed, and ask yourself the following questions:

- What does commitment mean to me?
- What did I do to support myself during times of challenge and frustration?
- Based upon past experience, in what circumstances does my commitment waiver?

One-on-One

Touchstone

On my thirtieth birthday, some colleagues worked together to create a framed photograph of Oprah and I standing together. It's actually the head of Oprah superimposed on the body of our company accountant— suddenly the *National Enquirer*'s alien baby photos make so much more sense! This photograph sits on my desk as a reminder of my commitment. What can you create that will serve as a touchstone, a physical representation of your commitment to your dream?

PART TWO
CONTROL

Why, why, why isn't this going my way? Have you ever wanted something so badly you can taste it? You work your ass off, you do everything right, and regardless of your determination it just simply doesn't go your way.

A few years into my career, I learned about the whole control issue first-hand. I'd identified my dream job at my dream company. After a telephone conversation and a quick perusal of my résumé, my "target" at the company called to inform me he was flying in from their headquarters for some meetings and would meet with me informally over dinner. I thought I had everything in the bag. I was ready. Over dinner we shared a few laughs, knew some people in common, and talked about our various achievements like peacocks—all great signs. Back home I marveled at the level of my desire. It outweighed anything I had felt toward my career before. I wanted the job, and I was determined to get it.

Finally, after a couple weeks, the verdict was in. The job was mine—I just had to be willing to move. Now, I would have done just about anything to get this job, but at this stage in my already complicated life, a move simply wasn't an option. I wanted this job, but I wanted it on my own terms.

Until that experience I really did have the sense that I could exert the upper hand in my professional destiny (I'd given up that illusion on the personal side a few years earlier). I believed with everything in me that if I wanted it bad enough and tried hard enough I could make anything happen. It hurts me to even have to write this sentence but here it goes—as much as we'd like to think we can control all aspects of our Quest, we can't. There are just some things that are not meant to be, regardless of our level of commitment.

> You know, you only have so much control over anything. So you can sit and worry and be miserable, or you can say, "I worked hard. Now let's see what happens."
>
> —Katie Holmes

As much as I wanted that job, I didn't get it—at least not the way I wanted it. It took a few days, but I slowly came to accept this reality and I began to look at some of the options that were sitting right in front of me, options I had been blinded to before. In the end, I was offered and accepted a job a hundred times better than what I was vying for.

It's one of those things we need to remember in the face of our compulsion to control. When your determination, commitment, and efforts just aren't enough to get you what you think you want, open your mind and your eyes to the opportunity and options that are calling for your attention. They are almost always better than you could have ever dreamed. As the Rolling Stones so aptly remind us, "You can't always get what you want, but if you try sometimes you just might find you get what you need."

Taking Time For Yourself

"I have to be out of here in an hour." Famous last words. In an effort to nourish myself with a little balance (got to practice what you preach) I decided to book a massage appointment in the late afternoon. Aware of my difficulty with the whole notion of relaxation, I fully disclosed my need to feel energized, not drained, and let the masseuse know I needed to be back downtown by 5:15.

My relaxed state crossed the line into comatose, but at 5 on the nose, my brain suddenly stood at attention, bolting me out of my stupor. As she marched past our designated time, I thought to myself, *Another five minutes won't hurt. See, I'm already better at this whole relaxation thing.* At 5:05, I tried to hoist myself up onto my arms to remind the masseuse I needed to be back at my office in ten minutes.

Apparently oblivious to both my request and the fact that my muscles were on full tension alert screaming "Get me the hell off this table!" the masseuse was still working as the clock struck 5:10. At 5:17, I had the pedal to the metal, infinitely more stressed than I was going into this whole "relaxation" process.

strategy*

THANK GOD

God, Buddha, Shiva—whatever it is for you, there's no denying a power greater than us exists out there in the universe. Consider the guy you were so certain was The One (he's now in jail), the apartment you coveted (it's actually rat-infested), or the job you want so badly (all new hires were laid off a month later). There is nothing better than looking back on your life to discover you simply couldn't have planned it better yourself! When facing something, anything, that just doesn't seem to be working out the way you want, immerse yourself in the following:

- Think about a time you really wanted something to happen in your life.
- What happened instead?
- How did this new alternative work out better than you planned?
- Thank God!

One-on-One

Let It Go

If you have a pressing problem, issue, or challenge—stop thinking about it. Sometimes the sheer force of trying to pop out an idea or solution works against the natural flow of problem-solving. Acknowledge the question or issue you're attempting to address and then let it go. Go for a walk, see a movie, or grab dinner with friends. I know it's hard to believe, but this seemingly simple strategy of not working, not trying to force an idea, actually works like a charm.

Highly driven women often ask about the difference between relaxation and laziness. Where's the line? How do you know when to have that third cup of coffee and keep going and when to take the night off? I've struggled to come up with an adequate response. All I know is that it ain't easy. When you're used to pushing hard, you may feel strange or even guilty when you stop and take a breather. There are no clear answers, but you will know in your heart where the difference lies.

Laziness makes you feel a little nervous, anxious—almost like you're going to be caught sleeping on the job. Instead, the only one who's going to catch you is you. Relaxation, once you let yourself actually enjoy it, feels good. Your mind settles down and lets go. You may even have brainwaves you didn't expect and your muscles unwind. Here's another way to think about it: Relaxation helps you get back in touch with yourself, while laziness drives you farther away.

PART THREE
CHOICE AND COMPROMISE

You're stronger than you think. Consider all the incredible things women do that are simply part of the job description. We can put up with a whiny boyfriend, contend with a bitch of a boss, endure forty-eight hours of labor, and pay to have our hair pulled out by the roots during a "pampering" session with our esthetician.

The power of commitment lies in one simple word: *choice.* When you choose to do something and use your will to see it through, you can do absolutely anything. Choice is vital because it inspires a sense of intention and gives you purpose to work through the hard stuff (and inevitably there will be hard stuff). Commitment is infinitely easier when you consciously decide to

---

✳ One-on-One

Hold Up

I'm all about not compromising yourself in the face of your Quest, but please remember—feelings of challenge and difficulty do not necessarily mean you are compromising yourself. I've seen a lot of books out there lately suggesting success should be effortless, that we should stop in the face of discomfort. Wouldn't that be nice?

There is definitely a strong feeling of "rightness" when you're on track, but when you are pushing the upper echelon of success, there are times of downright hardship and even distress. I've actually found more people compromise themselves by not trying hard enough, rather than by trying too hard. Sometimes short-term compromise is necessary in the pursuit of long-term goals.

Career Confession

THE NO-BRAINER JOB

I have the most boring job in the world. I sell advertising for a new magazine that has such a low subscriber base that no one will return my calls. Essentially I talk eloquently to machines all day. I am so used to being on voicemail autopilot, I can only imagine what will happen that fateful day when a real voice flusters me out of my cheerful phone routine.

Why stay, you ask? I am building something, a new business of my own, and I need all my energy for this new birth. Yes, I am bored at work, but the real fun happens in all the spaces in between, during my lunch hour, after work, and on the weekend. I am masterminding my dream. I have a business inside me, but I need to pay the bills until I am ready to transition my freelance clients into a full-time business. So this no-brainer job is, in fact, an investment in my future empire.

Jacqueline, advertising rep

focus all you've got on a meaningful, internally driven goal. And remember, you can always change your mind. Your dream is a living, breathing vision that will shift as you gain confidence and clear focus. Re-assess your commitments at regular intervals, and make any necessary adjustments. You always have a choice.

When A Good Job Turns Bad

You only have to consider the thousands of actors working in LA's bars and restaurants to know there's no shame and actually much use to

My whole goal is to keep my spirit intact. If that doesn't happen, none of this is worth it.
—Jewel

the "no-brainer" job. Just ask actress Halle Berry, who translated her serving experience into an Academy Award–winning role in *Monster's Ball*. There's something quite powerful that comes with choosing to work in a more fun, less thought-provoking environment while you build toward your dream career. While the no-brainer is often an important part of the process, the problem emerges four years later when you are still no closer to your dream. Here are a few pointers that might help you distinguish between the dream-job-maker and the dream-job-destroyer.

- **Not only do you not enjoy the no-brainer, you actually despise it.** "Hate" energy is just that—energy—and the more you waste on hating your job, the less energy you have to direct toward your dream.

- **Your no-brainer job eats at your sense of confidence and belief in yourself.** This often happens when you've been at it for too long. You start to believe that you can't do anything more than this, that no one would hire you for anything else. When your no-brainer starts to define who and what you are—instead of freeing you to live that definition on your own terms—run for the door.

- **Your body is sending you signals.** When I asked my actor friend this question she said constant diarrhea is always a key indicator. Although we can convince our minds that this is the right choice, our bodies are less willing to believe the lie. If you are suffering with chronic headaches or stomach upset, re-think your no-brainer.

- **Your no-brainer job saps all your energy.** This is the biggie I've found many people overlook. If you're an artist and work a "nine to five" to support your talent but come home exhausted and unable to lift a brush, this is a big sign. When you actually stop doing the dream work you've taken this job to support, get out.

When Your Choices Feel Like Compromises

There are times on the Quest when you will feel exhausted, frustrated, and downright nasty. Sustaining your commitment feels like a burden too big to bear, and the commitment to your dream feels less and less like a choice and more and more like a compromise. Although you will experience extraordinary highs on your Quest for Success, you will also experience some incredible lows—and most often these lows are attached to living at a pace of imbalance for too long. At times like these (we all have them) you need to nurture yourself. As much as you might not like it, you need to take some time off and get a little . . . balance!

If you find yourself repeatedly thinking any of these things, you have now entered the zone of perpetual imbalance:

- **Doesn't anyone else work around here?** You know you are entering into the zone of resentment when you are pissed off at everyone around you. No one works as hard as you do, and you are always the one left holding the bag.

- **No one understands.** You've become so tired and depleted that you've simply stopped talking. Usually you don't even notice you've stopped sharing your struggles and wonder why no one sees your need for support and understanding.

- **I don't know where to turn.** If you've been in a state of imbalance without asking for help for a long time, you feel in over your head. You don't know who to ask, how to ask, or what to ask for.

- **It won't hurt if I eat one more piece.** You've come to the point where you feel so deprived of pleasure, you feel like you deserve that eighth piece of chocolate and you most certainly don't have to go to the gym— you're working hard enough!

Career Confession

I HATE IT

Something miraculous happened the day I allowed myself to hate. The first day of my executive MBA program, I couldn't have been happier. I was so proud of myself for making the commitment, delighted to be surrounded by a new group of intelligent peers, and felt ready and more than able to take on this new challenge.

But somewhere in the middle of the semester, dividing my time between a high-pressure job and this rigorous academic program, I started to lose steam. I began concocting elaborate fantasies about how I would quit (suddenly, in the middle of an exam or just leave with no forwarding address). I tried to deny my feelings of frustration, exhaustion, and self-pity. I tried to scare myself into action with visions of dollar bills swirling down the toilet and my professional reputation in shattered pieces on the floor. What would I do if I failed? Nothing worked—I just kept on hating it. Then, suddenly, I faced the truth. I admitted to myself—this is f@#$%ing hard, I hate it, and I'm not going to pretend otherwise. Almost the moment I uttered these words aloud, I began to think about all the reasons why I loved the program.

Cynthia, student and management consultant

- **Pardon me?** You'll notice you've hit this plateau when your best friend is five minutes into a juicy story and you haven't a clue what she's said. If you are perpetually drowning in your own thoughts, too preoccupied to get past your own struggles and hear your friends, colleagues, and family, you've reached imbalance alert.

- **It'll get better once I _____.** Fill in the blank. At this stage of imbalance you are holding on to the future for dear life.

Respect The Bad Days

In the face of a long-term commitment, you have to accept that not every day is going to be a bed of roses and if there's anything you can't control, it's your feelings. Respect them. Respect your fear, your frustration, your sense of self-pity, and they become a part of your experience instead of defining it. When you give yourself the freedom to hate it—to have bad days—the good days are just around the corner.

> If it wasn't hard, everyone would do it. It's the hard that makes it great.
> —Tom Hanks

No, No, and No Again

Repeat after me—No. *Commitment* is really another word for *focus*. Your eyes are set firmly on the finish line and nothing, and no one, will stop you. Not even yourself. These are times when you need to circle your personal boundaries with razor wire. It's not about being selfish. It's about honoring your commitment and rejecting the tasks, people, and responsibilities that erode your rock-solid dedication.

> You do have to be fairly selfish when you have a gift. You cannot afford to let too many outside things get in the way.
> —Sarah Brightman

Here's another "no" for your repertoire: One of the bravest and sometimes most challenging choices (yes choices) you can make is to acknowledge you're not ready to make a commitment, that you're not ready to give it everything you've got. It's infinitely better for your sense of confidence and self-esteem not to try and convince yourself that this is the right commitment, the right time, the right choice—when quite frankly it just isn't.

In this ever-increasing world of push, you might decide to stay put. Success comes with knowing what you are comfortable with and defining your boundaries. Your decision, regardless of whether it's yes or no, is success in and of itself.

PART FOUR
COMPLETION

Post-partum, post-graduation, post-promotion, post-vacation, post-Christmas, post-party, post-date . . . Whoever said completion is the best part? Don't get me wrong. It's a fabulous, amazing, and exhilarating feeling to finish some-

---

Career Confession

AS GOOD AS IT GETS

I was always afraid to try my hardest, thinking I would reach or discover a limit that I'd rather not know. But I've learned there is something liberating about doing your very best and then letting it go.

I finally decided to apply myself to a major project at work, and I did everything—I mean everything—I could to pull it off. I ate (inhaled, really) sandwiches at my desk and worked until the cleaning staff tapped me on the shoulder and begged me to go home.

When the deadline approached, I started to panic. There were still so many parts I wanted to fill out and places I had hoped to brush with my sheer genius (in my head, this was not just a pitch—it was a Manifesto!). But I took a deep breath and told myself *At this time, in this place, this is the best I can do. Now I'm letting it go.*

It felt better than I expected. My boss was thrilled, but even if she had trashed my work, I wouldn't have cared. I knew I had given it my all, and I discovered the satisfaction that comes from knowing "this is as good as it gets."

Lauren, copywriter

thing—and to experience success after struggle. But soon, a nagging feeling inevitably comes knocking: "Now what?"

Pursuing a dream or a goal—or even an emotion-laden event like a wedding—is a satisfying process in and of itself. Sure, there are days when it's hardly heaven, but the goal becomes a companion. When you reach a milestone, you might also find a quiet but tangible void in your life. Feelings of grief, sadness, even anger are totally normal. It's an unavoidable part of the process, and your best strategy is to simply be prepared and willing to experience a whole range of emotions. And remember, you wouldn't have the post-whatever blues if you hadn't put your heart and soul on the line to get there. Feel proud of yourself— but stock up on tissues.

Giving Up

I was recently interviewed by another woman who was writing about women and success. She asked me verbatim, "What did you do differently than most women to get where you are?" Her question made me think. On my way into the office at 5:30 A.M., the roads dark and desolate, I decided it was a willingness to actually do what's hard. More specifically, it's having faith that just when it seems hardest, if you're willing to take one more step, success is literally waiting on the other side.

In the face of commitment, there is a time on your Quest when things will unquestionably get hard. It simply feels too intense, and the energy required to accomplish your goal or commitment is too much. What I've found is that if

> Just when the caterpillar thought the world was over, it became a butterfly.
> —Anonymous

you acknowledge the problems, feel your sense of discomfort, and decide to move on anyway, it usually takes just one incremental, difficult step forward to find a "sudden" breakthrough.

It's the fifty-million-dollar question: When do you keep pushing, and when do you give up and walk away? Although you are the only person who can really answer that question, here are some indicators that might help you reach a conclusion:

Indicators That You Should Keep Pushing

- You would be devastated if you gave up now.

- You think you're at the end of your energy, but the fire of desire still burns.

- It's worth the risk to keep trying.

- You're seeing progress, and your discouragement is just from feeling weary from the journey.

- You are scared and feel like a small girl in the face of a big challenge . . . keep going. The good stuff is coming.

- People think you are thinking too big. (I tend to think this is an early sign that something good will happen.)

- You feel overwhelmed by all you don't know and need to learn. This is normal. Just take it step by step.

Indicators That You Should Let It Go

- It doesn't have any heat. You keep plugging away, but nothing is confirming the direction you are heading. In some cases, it may be time to put it down or just reroute your efforts.

- It no longer fits who you are or what you want to accomplish.

- You realize that in order to achieve this goal, you're sacrificing everything you truly value.

- It doesn't hold a lot of meaning for you anymore. Remember, failure is succeeding at something that really doesn't matter.

- When you feel in your gut you need to give it a breather and come back at it with fresh eyes.

- Your most important relationships are suffering.

- You can't do anything more about it, and it has run its course.

- You are stubbornly holding on because you are afraid of what people will think if you stop, and you feel haunted by the concept of "failure."

- You are just doing it because you don't know what else to do.

- You are doing it to please other people and not yourself (i.e., your parents).

A mentor sent me an electronic document the other day called 21 Keys to Building a High Profit Business by Brian Tracy. Enticed by its title, I printed it to read at home over the weekend. Before Tracy heads into the twenty-one points, he opens with a doozie of a thought:

The inability to stop doing things that are no longer working and to discontinue people who are no longer performing, is the primary reason for failure in business.

Regardless of whether you are an entrepreneur or not, you need to think of your career as a business. Think about this concept again: Your ability to stop doing things that are no longer working is the foundation for building success.

I don't know about you, but when I first encountered this concept I felt a bit uneasy. Ask

> Hope begins in the dark, the stubborn hope that if you just show up and try to do the right thing, the dawn will come. You wait and watch and work: you don't give up.
>
> —Anne Lamott

yourself: Am I so invested and immersed in the direction I'm going that it's difficult, or perhaps uncomfortable, to consider an alternative path, solution, or objective? Commitment is a critical component for creating success, but there are points along the Quest when you have to be willing to accept—in fact embrace—the possibility that you could be doing something differently. Tracy suggests that we must learn to say three critical statements in order to examine what we could be doing better:

- **I was wrong.** Fully 70 percent of your decisions will turn out to be wrong in the end. The sooner you realize you are on the wrong road and turn back, the faster you will reach your destination.

- **I made a mistake.** The sooner you admit you have made a mistake and stop doing whatever it is that's not working, the faster you will move toward your real goals.

- **I changed my mind.** Always be willing to change your mind in the face of new information that challenges the old ideas or the established way of doing things.

✳ **One-on-One**

You Can Come Back to It

Making the decision to walk away from your commitment does not mean you will never come back to it. New opportunity awaits you and might directly or indirectly bring you back to this path at another point in time.

strategy*

ROSE-COLORED GLASSES

Almost as a sick way of ensuring we've really, *really* made the right decision, just as we finally, after months of internal strife, make our move to walk on, the universe places a pair of rose-colored glasses on our mental viewfinder. Suddenly, all you can remember is the one time your now-ex-boyfriend bought you flowers or your mind is stuck in automatic replay of the only compliment your boss ever dispensed. Here's how to keep your vision clear:

- Be prepared to support yourself through the inevitable rose-colored aftermath. Write down (before you decide to leave your job, boyfriend, or parent's basement) all the reasons you are deciding to walk on.
- Keep your list handy, and don't be afraid to pull it out for reference.

The Exit Strategy

My first quitting experience was a disaster. As I bravely sat across from my first "career" employer, I could just see the top of her head over the mountain of work piled around her. My speech prepared, I hesitantly began, "Margaret, I understand this isn't the best time to be leaving my position, but I've come to tell you . . ." What's that noise? Oh good God, she's crying. Her sobs got increasingly louder, and before I could go on she waved me out of her office.

There are two points in any job where you have the opportunity to make the most memorable impact: when you start and when you leave. Your exit strategy is a make-or-break situation. You don't want your employer to overlook your years of great work because she's stinging from your inadequate departure. Still a bit traumatized by my quitting experience (I actually swear that's one of

Career Confession

QUIT WHILE YOU'RE AHEAD

I'm sort of embarrassed to admit it, but I've quit—actually, I've quit three times—and guess what? I'm still working for the company. Why, might you ask? Is my voice broken? Can my boss not hear me? No and no. It's just that he keeps coming back to me requesting one more week, or he offers up a bonus toward the end of the month when my rent is due. I've caved so many times now that he tosses my resignation letters into the recycling bin without even reading them.

Annette, executive secretary

the reasons why I decided to start my own business), my mentor, Kirsten, shared some great pointers:

- **Break the news yourself.** While you should ask your new employer to give you a sufficient time frame to let your current boss know what's going on (two weeks notice, minimum), you'd be surprised how quickly news travels. You want to be sure your old employer hears the news from you first. Schedule a meeting with your soon-to-be previous employer ASAP.

- **Follow your "script."** Always meet with your current boss face-to-face and be prepared for an honest and direct conversation. Pre-think exactly what you want to say and actually write a script and practice it—quitting can be a nerve-racking process. If your boss sniffs a hole/weakness, he'll be after you with guns a' blazing. Be prepared.

- **Tie up loose ends.** After your conversation you need to do two things: One, write a resignation letter to follow your conversation, and two, create a strategy to make your transition as easy and beneficial to your old employer as possible. Lay out the situation: Here's the offer, why this is good for me, and why it's good for you (if at all possible). Come prepared with some sort of transitional plan. This is who can potentially replace me, this is how my work with the company can be wrapped up.

As bad as it is to be left behind, to be fired, or to be broken up with, there is something uniquely painful about being the initiator, the one who is actually responsible for the decision and has to be brave enough to walk on. As you come to the end of a journey, respect your own courage. Sometimes you have to walk on to ensure you can keep walking at all.

✳   ✳   ✳

If our obsession with yoga and cleansing diets is any sign, finding balance is a hot topic for schedule-crazed women everywhere. Equilibrium is a worthwhile goal, but I've come to grips with the fact that I'm never going to have a totally balanced life. Sure, there are days (maybe one Sunday last year) when I eat well, exercise, work a little, laugh a lot, play, spend time with family and friends, organize my shoe collection, and meditate. But most weeks? It's all about juggling priorities, and imbalance is simply reality.

The thing is, imbalance doesn't have to be a bad word. When you make a choice to commit to a goal, imbalance is a side effect of your unwavering focus. It helps you see what's truly important and to ditch the baggage. When I'm knee-deep in an exciting project and working day and night to see it through, I don't give a shit if my closet's a mess. Cooking? Who has time? But I know that once my intensive period eases off, I'll fill the cupboard, and my husband and I will whip the house back into shape. I not only choose to live with imbalance, but I use it to support myself through challenges. You can strive to take care of yourself every day and live a full, well-rounded life, but don't berate yourself when you have to buy a few more pairs of underwear just to make it to laundry day. Laugh it off and embrace the imbalance!

8

Do You Have to Choose?

Being a Woman in the World of Work

"Be real. If she were too pretty she wouldn't be considered credible. She has to be smart."

"I don't disagree, but you know as well as I do that she has to be considered attractive enough to watch. If this show's going to work she has to be easy on the eyes."

I had to interject, "Hey, you know I'm sitting right here?"

Three men and one woman look over at me, not the least bit surprised that I'm in the room, but obviously shocked at my apparent rude interruption to their conversation. Within seconds they are back into their heated discussion.

"I guess we have to ask ourselves where do we want the emphasis to be—brains or beauty. We have to make a choice."

Women face many questions and have to make choices that, let's face it, men just don't have to deal with. Brains or beauty? Kids or no kids? To date or not to date? To be a bitch or not to be a bitch (is that really an option)?

If there is one question that compelled me to dedicate a whole chapter to being a woman at work, it's this one: Why do women need a guidebook specific to them anyway? It's a question most often posed by a man, and I'm tempted to ask him, "When was the last time you had a conversation with one of your peers about the tick-tock of his biological clock?" Without question your career development depends on attributes that are not gender specific. Perseverance, vision, and excellence are not qualities that are exclusive to men or women. But the reality is, you will experience specific personal and professional challenges by virtue of being a woman, and denying this does a disservice to men and women alike.

Now, let's be honest. It's confusing being a woman in the world of work. And being a woman attempting to provide advice and strategies around these issues is even more confusing. If there is any chapter that I've lived and made mistakes through, it's this one. I have worn skirts that were too short, I've crossed the line with my boss, I am ambitious to the point of distraction, and I'd be lying if I told you I haven't used flirtation to get what I want. I've danced around this chapter for a long time for fear of saying the wrong thing. I still shudder at the memory of being caught red-handed by a fellow women's studies student holding a copy of Naomi Wolfe's *The Beauty Myth* in one hand and the latest issue of *Cosmopolitan* magazine in the other.

The goal of this chapter is to focus on the issues of particular interest to young women. This is an exciting time to be launching your career. Anything and everything is possible. Thanks to generations of brave women who paved the way, we have more choices than any other group of women before us. In the face of these choices, our responsibility is to keep the discussion alive; to share our perspectives, experiences, and knowledge; and to continue living our way to the solutions. We also owe it to ourselves—and to each other—to rally together around these issues. We need an implicit agreement not to judge each other's lives and choices. Despite all we have in common, every woman's Quest is unique.

This chapter is divided into the three hot topics that repeatedly come up in discussion with women from Seattle to New York:

- Dipping Your Pen in Company Ink—the ins and outs of dating at work.

- The Biological Clock Debate—when, if, and how will I fit children into my working life?

- The Power Shift—balancing work and relationships.

Career Confession

GONE FISHIN'

I started my career in the nonprofit sector. This translates into two important realities that affected my decision to give it a go within the private sector:

1) I was underpaid.
2) There was one man in the office for every fifty women, and guess what? We had fifty-one employees, and he was already taken.

Between working seventy hours a week and flopping into my bed-slash-couch to stare comatose at the TV screen, I made the critical decision—forget this! My real fear was not being poor; it was being single. All my equally career-consumed friends were meeting their significant others at the office and, well, I wanted to fish in the company pond, too.

After landing a position that excited me and suited my career development goals, I carefully chose my outfit for my first day—flirtatious or demure? Powerful or understated? As I entered my new office building, drunk with the energy that comes from being surrounded by powerful, confident, well-paid people, an attractive man held the door open for me. I smiled, thanked him, and wondered, maybe even hoped, he would be one of my new co-workers.

Carmen, corporate fund-raiser

PART ONE

DIPPING YOUR PEN IN COMPANY INK

Unless you work in a convent, the fact that you're logging twelve-hour days, six days a week will likely mean dipping your pen in company ink. There are a few things to acknowledge about dating at work—it's risky, exciting, and complicated. Whether you are single or already involved (this section covers both), the potential for your personal life to affect your professional Quest is certain.

Dating

We don't all come to work with visions of hearts and flowers, but it happens anyway. Work is where we spend our days, explore ourselves, and build our networks. Why would dating be excluded? That said, decisions around whether to date a co-worker or how to handle an in-office relationship are extremely personal. There are no right answers. There might, however, be a company policy. Legislation doesn't regulate matters of the heart, but you definitely want to understand the potential implications of a relationship with a co-worker. Find out how your organization views at-work relationships, and start your decision-making process from there. These tips can help you sort through both the emotions and the day-to-day realities of dating at work.

What's Your Intention?

No shame here, it's just important to acknowledge your purpose. The parameters of the relationship and the level of risk are directly proportional to your intention. Are you having a one-nighter with the company CEO to leverage a promotion? (High risk) Are you wildly infatuated with the boss you barely know? (Medium risk) Or have you developed a mutually supportive relationship with a co-worker you've come to trust and respect? (Low risk)

'Fess Up

If you think you can hide your affair from your co-workers, think again. I've worked with more than a few "undeclared" couples who thought they had the office duped. *Note:* Do not leave for vacation at exactly the same time, both return with a tan, and outright refuse to know anything about each other's whereabouts. Attempts to keep the relationship a secret usually fail and invite interest, speculation, and gossip.

First Stop, Top Floor

This might sound a little goodie-two-shoes, but my suggestion is to share your relationship with your boss first. Not in an "I'd like your permission" or parental kind of way, but rather in a "We've thought about this relationship responsibly and care about your business and our careers" kind of way. Inevitably, your boss will find out anyway, and you want her to be confident you will behave in a professional, ethical, and responsible manner. Your boss can even be an ally to help create personal and professional boundaries.

Nix the PDA

Blatant and indiscrete public displays of affection are difficult to stomach at the best of times, but for the sake of your co-workers, most certainly restrain yourself at the office. No one wants to watch you make out in the office corridor.

Use Discretion

If you've decided to date in the office, your days of coming into work to gossip about last night's Tantric sex session or wicked fight are over. Your new lover is someone else's co-worker or boss. Create some ground rules as a couple about sharing personal information with your professional peers. *Note:* Your onsite tech support might be enjoying your new boyfriend's racy e-mails as much as you are.

Even when you conduct yourself "by the book," you should know that your relationship may still change some of your co-workers' perceptions of you. For example, you and your colleague/boyfriend are sitting together in the company lunchroom and you wonder why everyone is opting to eat in their offices. Once you are attached to a partner at work, you might notice that others begin to avoid you, often with the best intention—to give you some space. In a new relationship, you might be excluded from invitations for drinks after work and conversations others fear you will share with your beau (especially if he's the boss).

While your dating relationship will inevitably offer a whole new experience of company culture, you might start to miss what you once enjoyed. The more you can sustain professional and personal boundaries, prove your ability to be trustworthy and discrete, and continue to retain relationships with other co-workers, the less you will miss out on.

One-on-One

Boardroom Table Club

And you thought the mile-high club was exciting! Before you decide to join the burgeoning ranks of the boardroom table club, consider this: If you get caught, you risk being demoralized, gossiped about, demoted, disrespected, embarrassed, and potentially fired. Is it worth it?

Career Confession

VULNERABLE

The company I work for is full of talented, creative, intellectual, and visionary people, but there is one man in particular who I've strongly connected with. Of course, he also happens to be good-looking, intelligent, and a charismatic leader. He really values my input and expertise, encourages the work I do, and repeatedly thanks me for the "remarkable" contribution I am making to the company. Now, who wouldn't be attracted to that kind of attention? At office social gatherings, we often end up in fun conversations about work-related opportunities, or even our personal lives and our families.

He is happily married with kids, and I am incredibly happy in my own young marriage. Never has there been reason to even think in a "flirting" kind of way, but I'm starting to sense a little something different. I find myself looking forward to the next time we'll work together, and I keep replaying his encouraging words over and over in my mind. I feel like I'm in high school again, with the popular boy paying attention to me!

Jamie, bank manager

The Affair

When was the last time your handsome, married boss came into the office, marched up to your desk, and whispered, "Hey, let's have an affair"? That's what I thought. Of all the women I've talked with about illicit office affairs, the most common opening line is, "It all started out so innocently . . ." Office affairs have a funny way of sneaking up on you, but I have some good news: There is a distinct pattern that, once deconstructed, you can begin to understand and control. The stakes are extremely high with an office affair. When you're single, you've got to take care of your heart and your professional credibility. When other partners are involved, you're playing more than just your own romantic hand. Keep your cards on the table and play fair.

Sparks Fly

You meet someone who sparks your interest. He appreciates your ideas, you make a great professional team, and he always says how smart you are and how great you look in your new suit. He might not be your usual type, but there is chemistry and he makes you feel alive.

You're Infatuated

There is a skip to your step and a buzz in your head—you have a crush, and at this point it seems fun and harmless. Your new flame is giving you the praise and conversations that you miss with your mate. In the back of your mind, you hear a faint warning bell, but this is way too much fun. You quickly hustle away the warning signs.

Welcome to Fantasy Island

You are now thinking constantly about this person. All of a sudden, you could care less if your boyfriend doesn't bother to call. You're too busy expertly contriving ways to bump into your new flame in the corridor and thinking up interesting yet provocative questions to ask via e-mail.

Let the Games Begin

You've been "bumping into each other" for a while now. Your confidence in this interaction is growing. One of you finds a way to let the other person know there is an interest. Think of it as a game of tennis. He might hit the first volley into your court with, "I so enjoy spending time with you." If you respond with

"I like spending time with you, too," you might find yourself engaged in a warm-up game, volleying subtle remarks back and forth during your interactions. Watch out. The intimacy level deepens and the momentum quickens with every volley.

You Cross the Line

At some, often indiscernible point, you've started having an affair. Whether it is purely emotional or emotional and physical, you've crossed the line and you know it. Actually, you knew long before you crossed, but now you have to face up to it.

Look in Your Own Backyard

If you are involved in a committed relationship and you find yourself attracted to a man at the office, the real issue resides in your own backyard. In all likelihood, you're discouraged, lonely, and feel taken for granted. On some level, you feel an emotional vacuum in your personal life. It has been a while since you really felt "seen" by your partner.

Dose of Reality

Okay, re-reading through this section, I'm afraid it looks like I'm proposing that we all go out and date the first colleague we can get our hands on. In reality, my goal is to acknowledge that some of us do, in fact, develop intimate relationships at work and to provide some direction beyond the most commonplace piece of advice you're likely to receive about at-work dating—don't.

Career Confession

ALL OR NOTHING

I just covered another napkin with my business plan. Confession: I am obsessed with starting my own business. I can see it in Technicolor. I really think I have what it takes. With five years of marketing experience under my belt and a rock-solid business plan, I know I have a shot. Here's my problem: I want to have a family. My husband and I have been married for a few years and I am closer to thirty than to twenty. Do I dive into the business only to pull up the tender roots in a few years and plunge into the world of diapers and play groups? How do I plan my life today knowing it will radically change in a few years? Do I speed up, slow down, change routes, split my dream, put things on hold, scale back, or compromise? Is it really all or nothing?

Kate, real estate agent

PART TWO
THE BIOLOGICAL CLOCK DEBATE

This is a hot topic that makes my own stomach turn. I will be walking down the street, encounter a baby, and feel at once scared (will I have enough time?) and desirous (how wonderful it must be to have a clear sense of contribution and focus). I keep making deals with myself—once the television show is launched, once the tour is over, once we settle into a home—the list goes on. Older friends and colleagues with kids pleasantly suggest there is never a right time to have children, and although I guess that's true, I know for certain there's definitely a wrong time.

I've yet to encounter a topic that makes young women sweat more than this one. Many young women are in the middle of a tug-of-war battle between family and career and wondering whether they can strike a balance between both. It seems we're all eagerly scanning friends, colleagues, and peers for examples of how it could work. From billboards to the cover of *Time* magazine, there's one message we simply can't miss: You'd better get the party started.

Watching The Clock

I engaged in two distinct phases in creating this section: a) the read-everything-you-can-get-your-hands-on, scare-the-shit-out-of-yourself, become-more-confused, theoretically-focused route, and the b) no-less-frightening-or-confusing, talk-with-women-who-are-actually-making-it-(or not making it)-work-in-real-life route.

It comes down to this: Discussions about the whole issue of women, kids, and work are fraught with challenge, controversy, and contradiction. The book *Creating a Life: Professional Women and the Quest for Children,* by Sylvia Ann Hewlett, was greeted with a storm of media attention and searing criticism. Considered a consumer flop with low-level sales on one hand but named among *Business Week*'s "Ten Top Books of 2002" on the other, the emotional reaction to this book clearly reflects the controversy surrounding work and children for women.

What's all the fuss about? Hewlett offers advice specific for young women eager to build a life that embraces both career and motherhood. She has definite opinions about how and when to start a family, which is an inherently loaded, personal decision. I sense an underlying tension—a level of deep-rooted frustration from young women who "hate" experts like Hewlett because deep down, we know there's some truth to her advice and we don't like it. It comes down to the fact that life is far stickier than any "expert" strategies might suggest. I keep returning to the same conclusion: You have to follow your heart and adapt any outside advice to your unique life and personal situation.

The following points offer a rundown of Hewlett's advice, and my own, real-world interpretations:

Hewlett Says: Figure Out What You Want Your Life to Look Like at Age Forty-five

What do you want your personal life to look like? What do you want your career to look like? If it turns out that you want children (and approximately 86 percent of high-achieving women do) you need to become highly intentional—and seriously proactive.

- **The reality: I can't even figure out what my life will look like next year.** When I was eighteen, twenty, twenty-two, I never even imagined I would be forty-five. It's not like I didn't believe the day would arrive, but I just couldn't picture it. Life takes twists and turns you simply can't imagine. Even when your goals and values remain consistent, life inevitably *looks* far different than what you had pictured in your mind. Think about what you want when you're forty-five—but don't count on a matching image when you get there.

Hewlett Says: Give Urgent Priority to Finding a Partner

This project is extremely time-sensitive and deserves special attention in your twenties. Understand that forging a loving, lasting marriage will enhance your life and make it more likely that you will have children. The data presented in *Creating a Life: Professional Women and the Quest for Children* demonstrates that high-achieving women find it much easier to find partners at younger ages.

- **The reality: If all I needed was a partner, I could start a family tonight.** In an ideal world, we'd all find our perfect companion at that delicate crossroads between sowing our wild oats and feeling ready for commit-ment. How often does that happen? A loving partner is wonderful, but don't forget that another person brings their own buffet of emotional issues and life goals to the table. You could find yourself with a partner who doesn't want children, who changes his mind, or who wants children before you're ready. The possibilities are endless. I don't want to scare you all the way to the convent—I'm just saying that a partner won't supply the answers. You're a smart, independent woman. There are many options.

Hewlett Says: Have Your First Child Before Thirty-five

The miracles of IVF notwithstanding, do not wait until your late thirties or early forties before trying to have that first child. As we now understand, late-in-life childbearing is fraught with risk and failure. And even if you manage to get one child "under the wire," you might fail to have a second. This, too, can trigger enormous regret.

- **The reality: My biological clock is already deafening. Thanks for turning up the volume.** One of my clients put it this way: "I grew up watching Jenny Jones and Ricki Lake show me the perils of teenage pregnancy—the food stamps, the loss of independence, and the emotional risks. Now that I've made it to twenty-four without accidentally reproducing, you're telling me to get the diapers ready? I don't think so."

  Don't get me wrong—I'm not debating biological realities. I'm just saying that fear (or an approaching birthday) shouldn't drive your decision-making process. Understand the risks and the options. Talk to your doctor about how you can keep yourself healthy and enhance your fertility.

Hewlett Says: Choose a Career That Will Give You the "Gift of Time"

Certain careers lend themselves to a better work/family balance because they provide more flexibility and are much more forgiving of career interruptions.

- **The reality: When did my fertility choices become wrapped as a Christmas bonus?** And where are men in this whole discussion? I know I've never met a guy who just started shaving and is now agonizing between a high-powered business career and a family-friendly dentistry practice. If those men are out there, I have one word: *hallelujah.*

Although it's a great idea to explore your options and think about the future, your choices should always come from a place of truth, not fear. Here's something else to chew on: You'll be a more tolerant partner, parent, and an all-around better caregiver if you're living your dreams. What could be a more inspiring example for your children?

Career Confession

I DON'T KNOW HOW I'LL DO IT

I always thought I had options. My parents, teachers, and professors all insisted I could be whatever I wanted to be. The sky's the limit. Glass ceiling? It doesn't exist for me. But lately I feel like someone was lying to me all along. I haven't planned my career (my life) around having a family. I've always known I wanted a family (if I find the right guy, if I get married, etc.), and I've always been driven to succeed in my career (good grades, good school, good job, promotions, etc.). But the two have always existed separately. Yes, I've thought about whether or not to work if I have kids, but I thought it was my choice, and I thought there were plenty of options.

The reality is, the sky *isn't* the limit. In my current job and industry, I simply can't work part-time. And I certainly can't take a few years off and expect to get hired again. Why didn't someone tell me sooner? But even if they had, should I have planned a different career path to accommodate a family that might not even happen?

Carrie, marketing executive

Career Confession

SHIFT FOCUS

Yes, when you have a child your life and priorities change—full stop. I'd be lying if I didn't admit that my child is my first priority in life. But somehow we've come to present the two options as if there is no in between. I love my child, and I love my work. When did it become a crime to admit both in the same breath? If I had to create a scale of love, yes, my child comes before my work, but they are not separate from each other.

In a way, having a child has created some much-needed boundaries in my life. A bowl of cereal for dinner three nights in a row doesn't cut it, and rolling home at 10 P.M. isn't an option. Having a child has enforced a new focus and established priorities I'm thankful for.

Lauren, financial planner

Hewlett Says: Choose a Company That Will Help You Achieve Work/Life Balance

Companies vary widely in the kinds of work/life options they provide. If you are an ambitious young woman who wants a family, find a job at a company that provides employees with a rich array of work/life policies that include reduced-hour schedules and various kinds of job-protected leave.

- **The reality: Why can't my choice be a world that actually supports women and families?** We're so used to walking this crazy tightrope that we don't even realize how screwed up it is. I know there's a big difference between an ideal world and the one we've actually got, but let's work to improve the situation. As young women, we need to use our power to create change. Women in influential positions can help institute corporate policies and a professional culture that truly values children. We need to involve men in the discussion and help them understand that without institutional support for working mothers—paid maternity leave, flexible schedules, child-care allowances—any talk of "family values," "children are the future," or "America's next generation" is pure bullshit.

One-on-One

Fantasyland

Sometimes having children seems like the perfect answer to all your problems. Finally, you'll escape the daily grind and find peace at home in charge of your own schedule, hanging out with your friends, catching up on your favorite TV shows, redecorating your house, and starting that long-delayed workout program. It would be like an extended vacation from work, but you would have this cute little person to dress up in adorable baby outfits and darling little shoes. Wake up! According to the young moms I've interviewed, this is a purely fantasyland view of motherhood. Maybe you're not punching a time clock anymore, but now you've got a new boss—your baby.

Trust Yourself

It's the strangest thing. Whenever I ask young women where they'll be in five years, they inevitably respond with one of two scenarios.

> **One:** I'm leveraging deals beneath a wall of black-and-white photos in my corner office and taking bi-monthly sales trips to Paris—flying first class and sipping Perrier. Oh, and I'll have a few kids.

Two: I'm hand painting a mural on the nursery wall, while little Emma and Isabella host a tea party for their favorite stuffed bear and Clarence the family cat. Oh, and I have a career of some sort.

Clearly, there's a gap in these crystal-clear visions. Young women can describe exactly how their career will look in five years, or how their family will look, but rarely do they have an image of how the two will fit together. And no wonder. Our mothers were the first generation to really combine career and family. If they wanted—or needed—to work after having kids, it was job by day, toddlers by night, and a conscience wracked with guilt about child care. Our mothers were trailblazers. Unfortunately, a generation later, the answers aren't much clearer. We're still struggling to figure it out.

> We still think of a powerful man as a born leader and a powerful woman as an anomaly.
> —Margaret Atwood

Not long ago, I was sitting in a planning meeting when a man suggested we integrate the concept of balance into a series of speaking engagements. Catching me in the middle of an eye roll, he asked, "What? Don't you have balance in your life?" Out of the depths of my body, with an energy totally disproportionate to the question, I snapped, "Balance is not a concept I have the luxury for. I'm thirty-three years old, and unless I want to be on this tour with a baby Snuggli attached to my Calvin Klein suit, I've got to give my work everything I've got—right now."

Juggling family and career goals is one of the most difficult personal choices women face. It's demanding, it's confusing, and it doesn't seem to be getting any easier. But as I've discussed this topic with pretty much anyone willing to listen and provide some perspective, a few conclusions have emerged. These aren't answers—they're simply the truths that I return to, over and over again.

First, although the waters are still murky, we will be the generation to find some clarity. We will help overhaul professional culture and create workplaces that support working mothers and families. And if the companies won't change, we'll

Career Confession

STORK-FREE ZONE

I don't want to have children. This is something I generally keep to myself, because otherwise people at work look at me like an alien who landed on their picket fence. I love children. I'm thrilled to spend time with my friends' kids, and I have nieces and nephews that I adore. I just don't see babies in my own future. Period.

Everyone always tell me, "Oh, I felt that way at your age, too. You'll change your mind." They smile knowingly. Well, I've *always* felt this way, and it would take a near-death experience to change my mind. When I see a pregnant woman, I wonder how many weeks until her get out of jail free card expires in the maternity ward. This is not the mind of someone who secretly covets fuzzy sleepers. I'm going to stick to pinstripes.

Jessica, publicist

build our own businesses. I'm not saying we all have to go out and revolutionize corporate America—good God, we're busy enough! But increasingly, we're not willing to put up with less-than-feasible working lives. We have more influence than we think—either they change or our boots start walking. As a Wildly Sophisticated woman, never underestimate your power and your options.

> I know that he [Matthew Broderick] doesn't have his laundry done, and that he hasn't had a hot meal in days. That stuff weighs on my mind.
>
> —Sarah Jessica Parker

Second, you can talk to every working mother you know. You can read books, scour magazines, and take undercover notes at your neighborhood playground. At the end of the day (and nine months), you have to do what works for you. This ain't easy. It's tough to start from scratch and create your own game plan. Everyone has her own social, financial, and emotional needs.

You have to take a hard, honest look at yourself and have clear discussions with your partner or your family. It's about your life, not Sylvia Ann Hewlett's.

And as I prepared to shred my copy of *Work Like a Man, Nurse Like a Woman,* I had a truly uplifting thought. By struggling to create lives that integrate both the corner office and the hand-painted nursery, we will build an amazing legacy for the children we're so eager to nurture. Our granddaughters can finally move past this discussion and actually enjoy those sales trips to Paris.

PART THREE
THE POWER SHIFT

I treated my marriage as the primary breadwinner. While I am more than comfortable in this role, I could sometimes sense a bit of tension in my husband. When the money topic would arise, I would wholeheartedly but somewhat dismissively tell him, "My money is your money." The balance changed when I started my own business. I no longer had a paycheck, and now our power shifted. Suddenly, I understood my husband's discomfort. Money isn't about money. Money is about control. It took a while, but I had to learn to trust in our relationship in a new way. My money and my career gave me a false sense of security—both personally and in my relationship.

From the conversations I've had with women across the country and my own personal experience, striking a power balance in relationships is an incredibly complex topic that could fill a book of its own. Our generation—for better or for worse—has watched traditional partnerships crumble into the history pages. Women today understand there aren't any guarantees or scripts to follow, and they often feel confused. Regardless of your personal situation, relationship power struggles challenge your core beliefs about independence, autonomy, and partnership.

Career Confession

WHO'S THE BOSS?

My strong, confident, and usually supportive boyfriend and I just had the conversation—okay—the fight of a lifetime. As I was packing my bags for yet another business trip, I casually reminded him to pick up the dry cleaning and asked him to transfer some money from my account into our joint checking so we could cover the rent. And then it happened—an explosion of anger and frustration indicating months, perhaps years, of repression. His list of beefs, ranging from the fact that I am always on the road to being left with the majority of the household chores, sounded slightly reminiscent of complaints I remember my mom expressing when I was a kid.

Taking some time to reflect on our conversation/fight, I've become increasingly concerned and confused. Although initially my boyfriend loved my independent spirit and commitment to my career, he has become aware (we both have) of the price our relationship pays for that kind of commitment. Can two equally driven individuals maintain a supportive, balanced relationship?

Kim, account manager

When my [future] husand proposed to me, he said, "Let me take you away from all this." And I said, "Away from all what? I'm a movie star!"
—Esther Williams

Who's on Top?

Just to make things a little more complicated, our current economic reality might require both partners to work full-time. Figuring out how to juggle income, child care, and about one hundred other factors can cause incredible headaches.

strategy*

Negotiating the power shift is all about communication. Whether you're just starting your relationship or have stuck together from first jobs to corner offices, it's an ongoing process. The following tips can help make your "couple life" run a little more smoothly.

- **Discuss your expectations first.** Long-term relationships change over time. Your expectations, wants, and needs will fluctuate, but there are some basic values you should have in common. For example, what does a committed, mutually supportive relationship look like?

- **Listen carefully.** If your partner is saying he doesn't want kids or he expects his career to take priority, believe him. Don't bet on changing his mind.

- **Watch for mixed messages.** Look for signs. Does he love that his sister quit her job to stay home and raise her children? What is his experience with his parents and immediate family? When he watches *Friends,* does he think Rachel shouldn't have gone back to Ralph Lauren and should care for Emma full-time (in between coffees at Central Perk, of course!).

- **Be real.** Discuss how to balance career priorities. Inevitably, you'll be taking turns. It's a tough issue and requires considerable vulnerability.

- **Make time for fun.** Remember why you're together in the first place, and keep things in perspective. Work can be a wonderful part of life, but life is so much more than work. Maintain a standing Sunday morning coffee date or Friday night chat over drinks. Watch old movies, walk the dog, or just generally spend some unstructured time together.

- **Get help.** Cleaning your house/apartment, fixing dinner, grocery shopping, doing the laundry—it can be brutal to work full-time and try to keep your life going. If you can't divvy up the chores in a way that works, look at using some of your entertainment funds to get help. The choice is yours— would you rather have a few nights of soup and sandwiches or spend all day Saturday cleaning the house?

If I had all the answers, this might be a very different book. What I do know is this: You have to know your own heart and forge your own path.

There's no perfect solution, only what works for you and for your partner. It's not easy to balance your vision of independence with life as part of a couple—but that's exactly what you need to do. If you're just starting to think about sharing your life with someone else, take the time to establish your own priorities first. Know where you're willing to bend a little and where your convictions are rock solid. This incredible self-knowledge will not only help you find someone who shares your own beliefs, but it will serve you well as you negotiate your own, unique power balance.

The Name Game

My friends and I have a ritual we call the Name Game. One of our entourage gets engaged and, you guessed it, we take wagers on who'll take their new husband's name. At first I thought this would be easy. Hoping to outwit my fellow

---

Career Confession

I DID

I had been dreaming of the day since I was old enough to actually spell my last name—the day I would get married and take my husband's last name. I had visions of Julie Smith, Julie Parker, Julie Peters running through my eighth-grade mind. Now, fifteen years later, I have just been proposed to. My thrill—not the wedding, not the dress, not the food—the name. Julie Mackenzie.

Julie, accountant

players, I created a foolproof checklist: Feminist stance (women's studies major), career ambition (VP level and above), difficulty pronouncing and spelling their husband's name (Zaharichuck).

I'm sad to say I'm down six to one. Apparently, there is no clear strategy for guessing whether or not someone will take a new name. The decision to take your partner's name is a deeply personal one and is influenced by a number of factors related to your head and, most important, to your heart. It's a choice that might involve practical considerations (i.e., a professional reputation you've built under your given name), religious beliefs, or family expectations, but regardless of influencing factors, always remember this is your decision to make. In this case, career strategies should take a serious backseat to your heart and your gut. Do what's right for you.

Career Confession

I DIDN'T

As I move through my marriage, more secure in its permanency (did I say that out loud?), I wonder if there wasn't a part of me that was a little afraid to take my husband's name for fear of having to change it back a few years later (hazard of being the child of divorced parents). Now, as secure as one can be in their marriage, I'm thankful I kept my name. Beyond actually liking my name better, old colleagues and friends from school know how to reach me and my professional reputation resides under one clear identity. I guess it all comes down to the fact that my last name feels like a part of me and, quite frankly, I wouldn't want to live without it.

Mona, lawyer

✳   ✳   ✳

Funny how insignificant the whole brains or beauty debate becomes in the face of all the other choices we contend with as young women. As it turns out, when it comes to brains versus beauty, there's really no choice to make after all. Although I can't be 100 percent sure, there seems to be a direct correlation between brains and beauty. The smarter, the more ethical, the more honest, and the more ambitious you become, the more beauty you exude. I've developed this fascinating (and heartening) philosophy by observing the Wildly Sophisticated women around me. I'm starting to realize that as you expand your mind, your definition of beauty changes. What's more, your external focus may shift in dramatic and striking ways. Tuck the latest issue of Cosmo *in with your feminist manifesto, and get on with your day.*

9

What Are You Waiting For?

Living Your Success Today

Colleen was nothing like I expected.

As a former Harvard journalism instructor and the editor of a highly respected Women and Management newsletter, I had decided Colleen would be my savior even before I met her. As she walked into the restaurant for our first meeting, I caught my breath. Colleen has an air of sophistication and elegance I've never encountered beyond the silver screen. She is a small woman whose presence fills the entire room, and just like her writing, she speaks deliberately and decisively. I still don't know how old Colleen is, but her carefully coiffed gray hair and persistent cough betray she may be in her seventies. Over lunch, we talked, laughed, and forged a connection.

A few years later, I found myself in the same restaurant, again sitting across the table from this brilliant, elegant woman. She looked me straight in the eye and grabbed my heart with both hands.

"Nicole, I have watched you thrash around with this idea for two years now. I believe in you. I wouldn't be working with you if I didn't. But you are the only one who can do this. I can't do it for you."

I took a deep breath, and before I could respond, Colleen continued. "What are you waiting for?"

In that moment, Colleen's question made me feel at once devastated and overwhelmingly relieved. I smiled. This woman, my savior, who I initially feared would be too soft, too lenient, was brave enough to ask the question no friend, no family member, and no colleague had dared to utter. With one direct hit, she drove her question straight into my core.

What Are You Waiting For? is the question that opens up the Quest. It offers a turning point—a pivotal moment of self-awareness and accountability.

One of my greatest fears is that you have reached this chapter and you feel totally bombarded with information. Maybe you're wondering if it's all worthwhile, or if you're any further ahead than where you started. Maybe you just want to go back to bed.

When I ask other young women What Are You Waiting For? the most common response is, "I'm overwhelmed. There's too much to do, too many choices, too many opportunities, and too many fears and questions in my way. I just don't know where to start." The truth? You've already started. You are living your journey, your Quest—right now. It's not something you have to wait to feel prepared for. You're here. You're living it in this very moment. You don't need to complete one single strategy in this book, you don't need your parents' blessing, you don't need a promotion, you don't need to finish your degree, you don't need to "accomplish," complete or *do* anything more—you are on your Quest right now.

I don't care if you're reading this on the subway, your parents' couch, or a rickety lawn chair adorning your empty apartment. Everything you are and have right now is enough. Just as the struggles you've already faced brought you to where you are now—bad hair days, empty bank accounts, self-doubts and all—this place and this moment is a crucial part of your Quest.

From material possessions to landmark achievements, our fairy tale is how we think we'll feel about our lives and ourselves once we grab that golden ring. We imagine that suddenly there will be no more fears, nothing but happiness, and every day will shine with love and perfection. Win an Oscar, and the path turns to gold. Sorry, but that's not the way it works. You will be the same person, with the same challenges, only now you'll have a statue on the mantel. Period. There's nothing more disheartening and disillusioning than struggling to achieve "success" and realizing, *This is not how I imagined it.*

> It's weird—when you're swimming in the glitter, it doesn't sparkle. You're just *in* it.
> —Vanessa Carlton

Don't get depressed. And please don't think *If success ain't all it's cracked up to be, now more than ever, why bother?* The challenge is to re-write your fairy tale. Success will be those shitty days when you want to crawl into a hole but you don't. It will be waking up and knowing you're living life from your heart. It's a moment. It's a feeling.

Okay, confession time again. My other fear is that this chapter will be too cliché. I remember attending an "inspirational" event for young women and hearing the smiling moderator sum it all up with, "Life is the journey, not the destination, ladies!" Give me a break! My blood pressure rose. *This is my life,* I thought, growing increasingly agitated. *I don't want it wrapped neatly into a cliché.* Once I calmed down, I remembered that cliché advice exists for a reason. Below all the tacky packaging is a diamond of truth. But I promise there won't be any New Age-y talk without solid and straightforward examples. And there won't be any more strategies that begin with the words "Close your eyes . . ."

You are at the foundation-building stage in your career. Don't sit around waiting to feel successful, thinking success is contingent upon one monumental achievement. The question What Are You Waiting For? compels you to focus on the successes you are creating day by day. This focus brings a sense of confidence and momentum to your career development. Wildly Sophisticated women focus on their strengths and create opportunities to realize success each and every day.

Self-improvement, growth, and learning are all critical elements of being a Wildly Sophisticated woman. What is too often overlooked and equally Wildly Sophisticated is the acknowledgment, acceptance, and celebration of where you are today—living in the now.

This chapter encourages you to focus on the present, focus on the positive, and finally asks you to focus on what you can do—what you are doing—today!

PART ONE
FOCUS ON THE PRESENT

I always thought that when we finally arrive at success, we move in, spread all our baggage around, and make it our own, never to leave again. I thought it would be this place you come to possess—our past a distant memory, our future a certainty. I was wrong. Success comes in one single moment—the moment in which you are 100 percent present in all that the moment has to offer. Success is created one moment at a time. It's not a place or a destination to be possessed. It's a lifetime of moments to be lived.

Expand Your Expectations

I've seen the thirty-year-old blues more often than I'd care to count. It seems we hit a critical birthday, one we've dreamed of from the time we were little, only to realize life didn't turn out quite the way we planned. Although this could be a potentially depressing realization, in reality it's the best news ever. Why? Because you now have the opportunity to reevaluate and redefine success, and you can attach it to the present instead of the future.

I think a lot of us are striving for something attached to an age, a possession, and/or a single accomplishment. It's almost that we're driving toward it, not enjoying the process or reevaluating if this "end" actually makes any sense to us anymore, and when we get there it's like *Oh. This isn't what I expected.*

I'm not suggesting for a minute that you lose sight of your goals. I'm just saying you need to live the process and keep your long-term vision attached to your everyday reality.

I challenge you to re-formulate your definition of success and look at it in terms of your personal mission. Rather than attaching success to an outcome or

Career Confession

I'VE ARRIVED

My thirtieth birthday. I've dreamt of this momentous occasion ever since I can remember. While others excitedly approach eighteen, twenty-one, twenty-five, I directed all my energy toward what I believed would be the turning point of my life. Actually, no, not the turning point, the arriving point.

I had visions of a happy marriage; a loving, handsome husband; a waterfront cottage in the Hamptons for the summer and a Manhattan loft for the winter; a glamorous career; and a wardrobe to match. Well, perhaps I should consider putting all my eggs in the big 4-0. I've dated a string of losers; my career, on its best days, only reaches the caliber of "job"; my wardrobe, while having smatterings of elegance, is primarily made up of Old Navy; and my apartment—let's not even go there. I thought it would feel different, arriving at this critical birthday. I've been holding my breath for a long time, wondering what this day would look like, and as it fast approaches, I'm afraid to exhale only to have to breathe in the reality of my life.

Barbara, travel agent

goal, could you look at it in terms of the process? I'll give you an example. Instead of saying success is a $100 million fashion empire, think of it as waking up every day and feeling great about what you're doing, working with people who inspire you, and creating the opportunity to learn more about yourself and the world around you.

Yes, have goals. You want to be an anchor on CNN, you want to make president of your company, you want to win the Nobel Peace Prize— these are fantastic outcomes to strive toward. But

> Getting what you go after is success, but liking it while you're getting it is happiness.
> —Bertha Damon

strategy *

A personal mission statement is a framework for living your life. It offers a structure and an articulated purpose from which you can make decisions and measure your true standards for success. Stephen R. Covey, author of *The 7 Habits of Highly Effective People*, describes a mission statement in these terms: "It focuses on who you want to be (your character) and what you want to do (contributions and achievements) and the values and principles that inform this personal road map."

Laurie Beth Jones, author of *The Path: Creating Your Mission Statement for Work and Life*, says a good mission statement should be:

- No more than one sentence long
- Easily understood by a twelve-year-old
- Readily recited by memory

Abraham Lincoln's mission was to preserve the Union. Franklin Delano Roosevelt's mission was to end the depression. Mother Teresa's mission was

without creating your own standards for success—and living them each and every day—you risk waking up with your goal in your hand and a hole in your heart. The strategy above will help you articulate your personal mission statement—a deceptively simple tool that keeps your dreams on course.

Give It Time

"Don't think I don't know you're cheating," my husband said as he kissed the top of my head and walked back to our room. Our first vacation in three years.

to show mercy and compassion to the dying. To create your mission statement, Jones suggests a three-step process:

- Pick three active verbs that excite you and reflect your intentions. For example: create, foster, explore, heal, enlighten, educate, and nurture.
- Articulate what you stand for. What principle, cause, value, or purpose would you be willing to defend to the death? For example: freedom, faith, service, family, dignity, excellence, and opportunity.
- Answer the question, "Who or what are you here to help?" You might answer: the sick, children, civil rights, art, the environment, justice, public safety.

Put the three steps together, and you've got your mission statement. Here's my personal mission statement:

*"My mission is to **inspire, support**, and **encourage** the **unthinkable** in **young working women**."*

Another great resource is Covey's "Mission Builder" tool on the Franklin Covey website (*www.franklincovey. com/missionbuilder/index.html*).

I had solemnly sworn that I would leave my work at home, and in all honesty, I fully intended to keep my promise. That was, of course, before I spotted *Martha Inc.: The Incredible Story of Martha Stewart Living Omnimedia* in the airport bookstore. "Hey honey, why don't you go get us a coffee, and I'll grab our magazines and meet you in the departure lounge."

I kept my treasure wrapped in a towel at the bottom of my beach bag, and just as Roy would slip into his mid-afternoon nap I would pull it out and voraciously read the story of Martha's compelling, complex, and long career. *Long* being the key. I have to tell you—forget the sun shining, the sound of the breeze rushing through the palm trees, the Caribbean sea in the distance, vacation be

strategy *

CELEBRATE YOUR OWN QUEST FOR SUCCESS

I swear that if there's any strategy you take away from the book, I hope it's this one.

Create a Career Journal. A scrapbook, reflecting the trials, success, joys, and accomplishments of your Quest for Success.

"It's going to take too much work." "Where do I start?" "I don't get it." I've heard them all. These will be your first reactions to this process. I won't lie to you. Initially, this strategy seems like a lot of work. But I promise that if you try this one, you won't be sorry.

What is it? A blank, hard-cover book destined to contain whatever makes up the essence of your Quest. A written description of your first day at work, your offer of employment, mean-

ingful quotes, pictures of your friends—the people who add depth and support to your Quest—pages pulled from your favorite magazines, memories of the hard conversation you were afraid to have but feel relieved to have over with, an e-mail from your boss congratulating your great work, rejection letters, your lessons learned. Track your progress. This strategy provides you with a way of documenting your journey, stimulating reflection on how far you have come, and, in turn, providing you the momentum you need to make your way into your future.

Still not convinced? I'll give you five amazing reasons why this investment is worth it:

damned—this was the best and, quite frankly, the most relaxing piece of information I had ever heard. Martha incorporated her business in 1977. 1977. More than twenty-five years ago! I don't know what makes us think success is somehow an overnight phenomenon, but what delightful news—it's not!

How often do you think to yourself *I wish I could get "there"* (wherever that is) *more quickly? Why isn't success coming more easily and effortlessly? Why does every-*

WHAT ARE YOU WAITING FOR?

- **It brings your Quest to life.** You are accomplishing more than you give yourself credit for. By actively seeking and collecting material evidence of your progress, you will find greater respect for your efforts. The images, words, and physical mementos of your own dedication gain drama and significance on the page.

- **You can't skip the buildup.** The struggles, failures, and challenges make you what and who you are. You will see—in photos and cards and scribbled napkins—that you've stayed true to yourself and your vision. There's no better way to appreciate your own courage and sustain your tenacity.

- **This journal is a celebration of your Quest.** It offers inspiration throughout the process and a tangible way to feel some healthy self-pride. It's the book you will rescue from a burning building.

- **It creates momentum.** Whenever you feel a bit stagnant, paste that recent airplane ticket in your book, and the next stage is under way. As you save and preserve the memories of your Quest, you're actually launching yourself forward.

- **It's a tangible record of *you*.** Picture this: You're ninety years old and the great-grandkids are circling your rocker on the cottage porch. Their attention drifts in and out as you read from your yellowing Career Journal. When you come to the description of that boss who pinched your ass, you can fondly remember that you once had an ass worth pinching.

one else seem to be having an easier time? *When in the world is it going to happen for me?* Beyond the exception of the Olsen twins, most of us are not born into "sensation"—it takes time, and time requires patience.

When I set out to write this book and build the Wildly Sophisticated business, I thought it would take me a year, two tops! Well, it took a hell of a lot longer than that. In a way, I think it's great that we underestimate the time it will

> **We detect rather than invent
> our missions in life.**
> —Victor Frankel

take to accomplish a goal. If I had actually known how long it would take at the beginning of the process—let's be honest—I probably would have opted for the "marry rich" route. Part of why we need to define success in the process, rather than the outcome, is that it just simply takes so much more time than we ever would have guessed.

Practice for the Big Event Every Day

Even without knowing it, so much of our daily activity, routine, and experience feeds into our Quest. It's not all about the big moments. It's about the little things we do to support and build our abilities for when life brings us the big events. Practicing to perform in the Super Bowl half-time show doesn't start a week, or even a month, before the event. Those performers have been practicing for the show in their basements since the time they were twelve. The big events in your life, whether you're presenting to a large group or supporting a loved one through a time of crisis, require practice. Think about your goals. What can you do today to start practicing for your big events?

Come Back Down to Earth

Like most people, I start my day with a hot shower. It's a basic getting-ready-to-go-out routine, but it's also one of my favorite moments in the day. There are no expectations when you step under the streaming water. I don't have to psych myself up or think *I'm going to have a really great shower this morning—maybe the best shower of my life.* I never worry, *Can I do it? What if this shower isn't as good as I'd hoped?* I just do it. It's one of those daily practices (and mindless routines) that bring me down to Earth. I polled some of my favorite Wildly Sophisticated women for their morning (and evening) must-do's.

I have to read the newspaper. I don't care if it's in a busy Starbucks or if I'm at home alone. I need a couple minutes with the paper every day.
Barb, personal trainer

A steaming hot cup of coffee. On really hard days, I swear it's the only reason I get out of bed in the morning.
Maxine, marketing executive

Even if it's only around the block, I need to take a walk every day. I'll leave the office just to come back to the fact that there is a world going on outside of me and my office.
Jocelyn, accountant

I know it sounds a bit crazy, but I love to ride the subway. I enjoy those first fifteen minutes of the day, sitting back and observing the fervor around me. I need these few minutes before I'm ready to dive into the day.
Margaret, architect

I love a hot mug of tea (not a cup and saucer kind of experience) in the evening. I put on my pajamas, wash my face, and sit down to reflect on the day.
Heather, mom

I pray.
Patricia, business owner

I love to sink into a hot tub of water at the end of a long day. It's my time and place for myself and myself only.
Janice, financial planner

I start my day with some music. I love to get ready to the sound of my favorite artists.
Jennifer, freelance writer

Career Confession

DRINKING IN LIFE

I was walking past the great vintage/secondhand/junk shop in my neighborhood the other day when I noticed a new album on top of the pile—Engelbert Humperdinck, *Release Me.* With his head turned in profile and his eyes narrowed in seductive contemplation, he looks kind of like a young Brit-pop hipster.

He was really hot in his day, I thought to myself as I walked to the bus.

As a journalist, it's my job to capture and interpret the world for an audience. I bring simple experiences of everyday life—large and small—into my work. I don't know when I'll write about Engelbert, but I do know that day will come and I'll draw on this goofy little moment. Life is so textured and rich. You simply have to drink it in.

Julia, reporter

PART TWO
FOCUS ON THE POSITIVE

I know you know those days—your boss is on your ass for the report you can't seem to get your head around, you've spilled coffee down the front of your new linen suit and you've got an investor meeting in an hour, you've come to nickname the ringing of your phone the Devil's Siren—and it won't stop screaming your name. I was having the day from hell. Nothing but nothing was going right. My secretary gently rapped on my door to find my head on my desk as she delivered a conspicuous looking FedEx package. I halfway thought *Ah, to make my day complete, divorce papers from the husband I only remember from the picture on my desk.*

Reluctantly, I opened the legal-size envelope to find another card-size envelope, and inside that envelope another ten miniature envelopes. What could this be? I recognized the handwriting immediately, my best friend Jenn. She had sent me ten "Appreciation Cards," from "I love your voracious need for knowledge and your love of books (not to mention the ones you pass on to me)" to "I appreciate your adamant stance that life will be fun and full and exciting—and I love how that influences me." It's the best gift I have ever received in my life.

How could I, for one single, solitary moment, think of anything more than how great life is? You don't need to receive appreciation cards (in fact, it's more helpful to send them) to focus on the positive in your life. No matter how bad or hard or challenging the Quest can become, never, ever forget all the positive things your life contains—and you are on the top of the list. You are an amazing young woman, at one of the most exciting junctures in your life. You have the opportunity to give thanks for all you have been given in this world, and with that foundation of gratitude, you have everything you need to live your Quest.

The more you look at the world in wonder, the more abundance you feel in your heart, and the more thanks you give, the more you receive. It's sort of hard to describe, but it's like when you say thanks to the Universe, it's so happy to be acknowledged that it keeps giving you great things. It's like someone saying, "Well, you liked that one, let me show you this!"

Cultivate Gratitude

If you haven't read Sarah Ban Breathnach's *Simple Abundance: A Daybook of Comfort and Joy*, go out and get it today! One of the most powerful principles she discusses comes on January 13, and on the very next day she suggests how you can bring the powerful principle of gratitude to life.

> *January 13: When I surrendered my desire for security and sought serenity instead, I looked at my life with open eyes. I saw that I had much for which to be grateful. I felt humbled by my riches and regretted that I took for granted the abundance that already existed in my life. How could I expect more from the Universe when I didn't appreciate what I already had?*

> *January 14: This first tool could change the quality of your life beyond belief: it's called the Gratitude Journal. I have a beautiful blank book, and each night before I go to bed, I write down five things that I can be grateful about that day.*

Maintaining relationships with family and friends is hard when you're really busy. When you're younger you don't think about it as much. You sacrifice it for a few years and then you realize, "What the hell am I doing?"

—Jennifer Lopez

Hold On to Friends and Family

There's nothing like coming home after landing the biggest account of your life. Millions, no, billions of dollars at stake, a global software company signing on the dotted line and accepting your marketing proposal. Now imagine unlocking the door to a completely empty apartment. No friends to toast your success, no partner waiting with

Career Confession

NO FRIENDS

Another long day at work, Chinese take-out in hand, I check my voicemail. Hmmm . . . nothing. Again. I think back to the last time I have had a call from anyone besides my mother. Good Lord, do I have any friends anymore? I grab a pad and paper and make a list. Shelly, Lauren, Brooke, Katie. My heart stops . . . I can't remember the last time I talked to any of them. They used to call and invite me out, but let's face it, with traveling and work I hardly have time to go anymore.

I must have a few more friends. I begin flipping through my Rolodex . . . of course, Kelli. Oh no! I forgot Kelli's birthday. Is it today? Was it last week? I tear through my closet for a recent purchase I could hustle over to her as a birthday gift.

I am such a loser friend. Who am I kidding? I don't think I even know my friends anymore, and I wouldn't know what to talk about even if I did. Everyone's eyes glaze over when I talk about work. And I can't participate in their conversations. What's the deal with *Survivor*? All that bug-eating and camping sounds dreadful.

I flop dramatically onto my bed. Face it. I'm going to die a lonely, pitiful death in an apartment full of cats. I dial up my mother . . .

Susan, financial analyst

roses, and no supportive family members a phone call away. Depressing, no?

As you strive to achieve greatness and grab hold of your dreams, don't forget who's there holding your hand. Your Quest will lose all its meaning if you sacrifice your relationships for an ultimately empty definition of success.

Remember what and *who* is truly important in your life. Make the needs of your loved ones a top priority. Make adjustments and sacrifices wherever you

> **We never really stop to think about how amazing it is that we do the things we do every day—until we're not able to.**
>
> —Niki Taylor

need to. Think about what sort of home life and environment you want to create for yourself and the people you love. Decide what kind of relationships you want with family members, friends, and partners, then take action to build and nurture those ties.

Get Some Perspective

My friend Beth had been down in the dumps for weeks. A bad breakup and an unexpected layoff put her life into a tailspin—all understandable for the first month afterward, even the second, but as the third month of melodrama raged on, I invited her to come along with me to my great-grandmother's old-age home. Four hours later, as we emerged smelling of that unique concoction of antiseptic/urine/bleach, Beth turned to me unprovoked and declared, "You know Nic, if nothing else, I can wipe my own ass."

On most days, we don't need to fixate on the hardships of others to put

---

❋ One-on-One

What's Going Right Instead of Wrong

Having a bad day? We all have them. Give yourself five minutes to rant. Write down every single little thing that is pissing you off and not going right. Get it all out. Then when you feel spent, bring your attention wholly and completely to the positive. Write down every single thing that's going right. Although it might have taken you a bit longer to get started on the positives, you will have infinitely more significant things going right in your life than going wrong.

our Quest into perspective, but if needed, a trip to your local food bank, hospital, or old folks' home will do the trick.

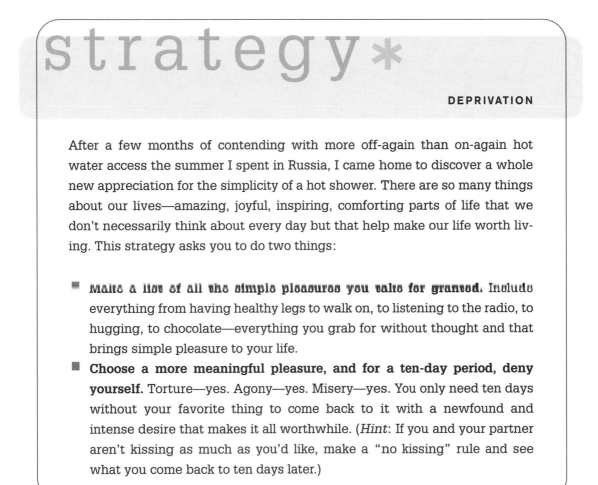

strategy*

DEPRIVATION

After a few months of contending with more off-again than on-again hot water access the summer I spent in Russia, I came home to discover a whole new appreciation for the simplicity of a hot shower. There are so many things about our lives—amazing, joyful, inspiring, comforting parts of life that we don't necessarily think about every day but that help make our life worth living. This strategy asks you to do two things:

- **Make a list of all the simple pleasures you take for granted.** Include everything from having healthy legs to walk on, to listening to the radio, to hugging, to chocolate—everything you grab for without thought and that brings simple pleasure to your life.
- **Choose a more meaningful pleasure, and for a ten-day period, deny yourself.** Torture—yes. Agony—yes. Misery—yes. You only need ten days without your favorite thing to come back to it with a newfound and intense desire that makes it all worthwhile. (*Hint*: If you and your partner aren't kissing as much as you'd like, make a "no kissing" rule and see what you come back to ten days later.)

Have Fun

With this book weighing heavily in your hands—just one more thing—have fun. I know. When and where did fun become yet another obligation? "I don't have time to have fun!" our mind screams, while our subconscious dances with delight. Having fun doesn't have to become a chore; it only feels that way when we've gone too long without it.

Does having some more fun sound wonderful but you don't know where to get started? I asked some of my Wildly Sophisticated friends and colleagues to share what they do for a roaring good time.

Flirting

Going to a movie

Discovering somewhere new

Dining out with great friends

Playing with my dog

Playing a game of Frisbee

Spending an afternoon of pampering at the spa

Kissing

Doing handstands against a wall

Laying in the grass in the sunshine

Skating—either roller or ice

Finding $2.99 breakfast specials

Doing something I'm not supposed to do

Watching dogs (my partner and I make up voices for them as they sniff each other's bums)

Enjoying a day of movie rental in bed with some ice cream

Doing anything with my hands

Playing any kind of sport I suck at (no pressure to be perfect)

PART THREE
FOCUS ON THE POWER OF POSSIBILITY

"So how did you get this gig?" I couldn't help but ask after our interview was over. This was an obviously bright young woman, but I imagined there must have been a line a mile long for the position of staff reporter on the school newspaper. "It's funny," she replied. "The posting went out via e-mail

Career Confession

FORGOTTEN WHAT FUN MEANS TO ME

Another lonely meal out on the road. I sit in the hotel restaurant in my slightly rumpled business suit picking at my salad. Tired of reading the novel I picked up at the airport gift store, I glance out the window overlooking the hotel pool. I am transfixed. Four young girls are putting on what seems to be their own synchronized swimming contest. They are horrible, yet they are pulling out all the stops and it is hilarious. At one point they are all hanging on to each other and trying not to drown because they are laughing so hard.

So that is what fun looks like. I forgot.

To be honest, I can't even remember the last time I laughed so hard I felt weak or experienced that giddy euphoric sensation of thoroughly enjoying myself. My nights out consisted of business cards, handshakes, and the predictable networking small talk. Nights in are equally bland—take out, TV, and my dog, Barkley.

Somewhere between mergers and acquisitions, I forgot how to have fun.

Lisa, sales executive

to all the students here at the college. My initial inclination was to not bother applying, thinking so many others would beat me to the punch. But I did, and the funny thing about it is my boss later told me that only five people actually applied."

Later that afternoon, I talked with a group of the reporter's fellow students and asked them if they remembered the posting. Everyone nodded their head yes. I then asked if anyone was interested in applying. Almost seventy hands shot up.

The greatest of all mistakes is to do nothing because you can only do a little. Do what you can.
—Liz Smith

"Why didn't you apply?" I was curious to know. One brave soul uttered his brave reply, "I thought there was no use."

Please hear me when I say this: In times of high unemployment rates and in the face of a highly competitive application process—get out there! Why? *Because the majority of people have given up without trying.*

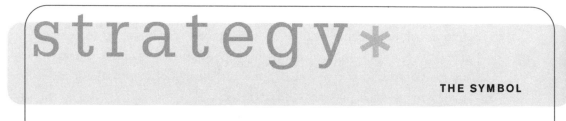

strategy*

THE SYMBOL

Actor Jim Carrey wrote a million-dollar check and put it in the pocket of his father's jacket before he was buried. Jim was not yet a millionaire. Gerri Halliwell of the Spice Girls wrote down her goals on the back of a picture of herself as a young girl. The list included being part of a world-famous pop band. Sarah Ban Breathnach, author of the Simple Abundance series of books, took a *New York Times* bestseller list, whited out the title in the number one spot, and typed in *Simple Abundance*. The book hit number one on the *New York Times* bestseller list two months ahead of schedule.

What can you do today to symbolize your belief in yourself?

Don't Play the When/Then Game

Susan Jeffers, author of the book *Feel the Fear and Do It Anyway,* has a philosophy she calls the When/Then game. Jeffers explains the game as, "When I feel better about myself . . . then I'll do it." She continues, "This is a mix-up in the order of reality. I kept thinking that if I could improve my self-image, then the fear would go away and I could start accomplishing things."

The fundamental essence of Wildly Sophisticated demands that success is in the process. This means before the promotion, before you get the raise, and before you take the leap to start your own company, your words and actions have to convey your belief that you deserve success, that you are successful. If you intend to be the CEO of a company, act the part, dress the part, and live the part today.

It's easy to get into the "save-it-for-later" syndrome. You know what I'm talking about—the beautiful suit you love but don't want to wear out, the candles you're waiting for just the right time to burn, the spa gift certificate that seems too indulgent to use this week. Possessions often symbolize our hopes and dreams, and saving them for later is just another way to hit the pause button on life. Put on that gorgeous party dress, crack open the 1999 Merlot, and start celebrating *now.*

> **Good is the enemy of great.**
> —Jim Collins, *Good to Great*

One-on-One

Passing Up Good for Great

It takes faith to believe wonderful things are available to us. We often think we should just be grateful to have the work, boyfriend, or life that is "good enough."

Never undersell yourself. To pass up good for great, you'll need to develop the patience and emotional strength to sit with wanting something that's good (like a new job) while you pursue something that's great (the right job that utilizes your best talents and skills). This will be challenging at first. We live in a society that reinforces instant gratification. Fortunately, the more you use patience, the more patience you'll have, and the easier it will be to hold on until you find what's truly great.

Spin Straw Into Gold

Some of the world's most powerful, influential, and intriguing people got that way not because they are perfect, but because they are flawed. These people stand out from the flock because they draw on their challenges to build strength. For example, Michael J. Fox shocked fans and followers in 1999 when he admitted he had been battling Parkinson's disease since 1991 and could no longer hide the symptomatic tremors. Here was this handsome, successful man who suddenly became "real." He has since gone on to launch the Michael J. Fox Foundation for Parkinson's Research and take on occasional directing and acting projects. He was not immune to challenge and has since become a model of courage, commitment, and generosity.

> How do you build credibility? Not by pretending to be perfect, but by being honest.
> —Rick Warren, *The Purpose-Driven Life*

People who are vulnerable do not look weak—they are actually more attractive. Don't deny your flaws or worry that they will prevent you from achieving success. Use what you've got. Work it!

Build Your Reserves and Nurture Yourself

The music is soft, the lights down low. Brad Pitt is slowly pushing strands of perfectly highlighted hair back from my face. He gently lifts my chin, looks deep into my eyes, and is about to kiss my full lips when all of a sudden, we hear a chain saw rumble somewhere in the distance.

"Never mind, Brad," I coax him, bringing his attention back to me. His lips are now gently brushing mine. He begins unbuttoning my Prada blouse, exposing my exquisitely tanned shoulder. He nuzzles his fresh-smelling face into the nape of my neck when . . .

"What the f★%$# is that noise?"

I break from his embrace, determined to find the source of distraction. I find the noise alright. I sleepily come back to reality to find my husband, mouth wide open, snoring like a dog.

Nurturing yourself and your strengths on the Quest is a critical part of creating success. A good night's sleep, a blow-dry on a particularly stressful afternoon, a matinee movie when no one's looking—nurture yourself and build your reserves.

Sleep

A good night's sleep is a necessity, not a luxury. Your noisy neighbors, the cat that keeps jumping on you in the night, your snoring boyfriend, your screaming baby—you think you're invincible until you face a couple sleepless nights. Sleep plays an essential part in preparing your body and mind for optimum performance. And research shows that even a slight loss of sleep can have a significant impact on our mood, productivity, communication skills, and general health.

Are you getting enough sleep? If you regularly log less than eight hours of sleep each night, fall asleep instantly, or need an alarm clock to wake up, you could be one of the 63 million people in North America who are moderately to chronically sleep deprived. As you sleep, your brain is performing important physiological, neurological, and biochemical tasks. These tasks are crucial to your overall health, as well as your ability to remember and organize your thoughts.

Grab a Moment

You know you're in trouble when the sun on your face feels like a foreign lover's gentle touch (still thinking about Brad). I was running from one meeting to the next and suddenly felt the warmth of the sun. All it took was one single minute to slow down—to actually feel the sun and remind myself what it means to live life—and then I went on to my next meeting. Work with what you've got. No, not every day is 100 percent your own. You have responsibilities and commitments that require your attention, but don't forget to pay attention to yourself. Work a few moments of slow motion into your feverish pace.

Laugh

When was the last time you laughed out loud? Not the *yeah, that's a good one* kind of laugh; the side-splitting, can't breathe kind of outburst that makes you feel your abs again. What makes you laugh out loud?

Put It Down

Quite literally—drop it. If you're known around the office as "the bag lady," dragging along your collection of briefcases, laptop, and purses—put them down. Lots on your mind? Get out a pen and a notebook and write down every single thing that is pissing you off, confusing you, or making you sad, frustrated, and lonely. Put it all down. If you find your shoulders wrapped around your ears (and it's not −20 degrees) bring those babies down, too.

Relax

Sometimes it feels like you'd need a month on an island spa retreat to actually make up your sleep debt and relax those anxiety-ridden muscles (and that's not in the budget or schedule). In reality, waiting for a big trip to start pampering yourself is a mistake. Relaxation does not have to be a major investment of time or money, and, in fact, if you give yourself little indulgences, you're less likely to hit crisis mode (requiring lots of time and lots of money—think of it as an investment). There are tons of little things you can do to make your Quest more enjoyable and take care of the most important asset you have—you.

> **Your playing small does not serve the world. There is nothing enlightened about shrinking so that other people won't feel insecure around you.**
> —Nelson Mandela

Make A Difference

Step outside yourself for a moment and think about your work. How does it affect other people? How are you helping? Making a difference? It's a common mistake to think of ourselves as small and powerless. The reality is very different. Everyone—regardless of occupation or status—affects the world through the work they do.

Think about a mail carrier. Simple job, right? Develop awesome legs as you walk a standard route and drop off letters. But consider the different pieces of

strategy*

DO SOME GOOD

Choose a cause you feel passionate about, and offer a helping hand. This isn't necessarily about signing over a check. Stuffing envelopes or handing out fly-ers—it all makes a difference. By exploring your ability to make an impact "out-side" your life, you directly affect the feelings of efficacy "within" your life. It's easy to believe we are too small to create change, waiting until we have more money, more power, or more time. This is simply not the reality. Power lies in acting on your passions today—and using whatever you've got to give.

- **Pick a cause you believe in, or an issue that raises your temperature.**
- **Figure out what you can do to contribute or raise your voice.** Write let-ters to government officials, serve meals at a homeless shelter, or read to kids in the children's hospital.

mail a carrier delivers every single day: birthday cards, congratulatory notes, bills, college acceptance letters, a new credit card. Imagine how all these items influence people's day-to-day lives. Suddenly, a simple job takes on greater weight.

Or maybe you're a secretary. By keeping an office organized and answering phones, you're supporting the organization's larger purpose, caring for your bosses' and co-workers' needs, and offering a human face to everyone who visits the office.

Thinking about your work in the "bigger picture" is a great way to gain perspective and understand how interconnected the world really is. You are powerful right here and now.

✳   ✳   ✳

What am I waiting for?

In my mind I debated, Do I tell Colleen the truth? *Do I tell her about the afternoon of my thirtieth birthday when I sat down with my checklist of goals and scratched off Range Rover, six-figure salary, VP level executive, board member, and married, then cried because I had never felt less fulfilled? Do I tell her that I often feel overwhelmed by the choices I am presented with—afraid to make the wrong one? Do I tell her about the arguments my husband and I have that always seem to incorporate the words* work *and* resentment? *Do I tell her about how badly I want to have children some day? How I worry I will be too old to conceive by the time I have this career thing down? Do I tell her how happy it makes me to think about career development and the exhilaration I get from working with young women? Do I tell her I am afraid to write because I am afraid I will fail, and I am afraid I will succeed?*

We finished our lunch and I got in my car. Three blocks down the street, I pulled over and took out my phone. I booked a trip to the coast and gave myself four silent days to sit with Colleen's question. In truth, I already knew the answer. I had known the answer even before I heard the question. What was I waiting for? Nothing. There was nothing and no one holding me back, and on my trip, I finally began to act. Colleen's simple, pointed question—what are you waiting for?—had compelled me to leap.

Now it's time for me to give you a push. You've already started. Your dreams are rich and full within you.

What are you waiting for?

Afterword

It's a beautiful spring day. After weeks of rain, the sun has emerged, and I'm sitting under a blossoming pear tree wondering why my iron-clad will is not enough to push out this conclusion. The book has been edited and my final task is to write a few last paragraphs, which, quite frankly, should be a breeze for me at this point. But somehow, I just can't. As I lay on my back looking up at the sky, I ask myself, "Why . . . why . . . why is this so hard?" And then it hit me.

I don't want it to end.

I've put so much of my life on hold—what will I return to find? How will I spend my sleepless nights if I'm not thinking about what to write? What will I do next? In these questions, I captured the single most important part of the Quest—it never ends. All we have to do is ask the questions again: Who Do I Think I Am? Am I Prepared? Do I Have to Choose? Only the questions remain constant; it's our answers that change as we continue to grow, evolve, and learn through our life.

Just as the Quest never ends, it never really begins. If you are as afraid of starting as I am of finishing, what we both need to remember is that we can't get on or off this train—we're living the Quest right here, right now.

Your career is an incredible key—two keys, actually—one to yourself and one to the world around you. I'm not quite sure if you can separate your personal and your professional life, and I guess my question would be, do you really want to? You can do anything in this world. You can achieve the extraordinary.

If you can dream it, it's possible. If there is anything this writing process has taught me, it's that even your greatest unthinkable is achievable once you face the questions and live through your own unique solutions.

Live your Quest with all your might, all your heart, all your mind, all your resources, and all your talents. This is your life and your journey to realize. The Quest for Success is amazing and it's yours. Reach out and grab it.

Index